The Book of Treasure Spirits

The Book of Treasure Spirits

Being a partial transcription of material from Sloane MS 3824, dated 1649, and containing material originally bound together with part of Sloane MS 3825, including a conjuration of the spirit Birto said to have been performed at the request of Edward IV, King of England. The relevant part of MS 3825 is available as *The Keys to the Gateway of Magic* (Golden Hoard Press, 2005) by Stephen Skinner and David Rankine.

For further details of *The Keys to the Gateway of Magic* which is Book II of *The Sourceworks of Ceremonial Magic* series by Stephen Skinner and David Rankine, edited from rare classical manuscripts see:

www.avaloniabooks.co.uk or www.goldenhoard.com

OTHER BOOKS BY THIS AUTHOR

BOOKS BY DAVID RANKINE
CLIMBING THE TREE OF LIFE
CRYSTALS HEALING & FOLKLORE
HEKA ANCIENT EGYPTIAN MAGIC & RITUAL
BECOMING MAGIC

BOOKS BY DAVID RANKINE, WITH SORITA D'ESTE
HEKATE LIMINAL RITES
THE ISLES OF THE MANY GODS
VISIONS OF THE CAILLEACH
THE GUISES OF THE MORRIGAN
PRACTICAL ELEMENTAL MAGICK
PRACTICAL PLANETARY MAGICK
CIRCLE OF FIRE
WICCA MAGICKAL BEGINNINGS

BOOKS BY DAVID RANKINE, WITH STEPHEN SKINNER
A COLLECTION OF MAGICAL SECRETS
PRACTICAL ANGEL MAGIC OF DR JOHN DEE'S ENOCHIAN TABLES
KEYS TO THE GATEWAY OF MAGIC
THE GOETIA OF DR RUDD
THE VERITABLE KEY OF SOLOMON

"The first thing the Magical Philosopher is to observe herein, is to be well informed, or well to inform himself by all the best ways & means he Can, whether by any Treasures are hidden in Such or Such a place or no, and by whom"

The Book of Treasure Spirits

A grimoire of magical conjurations to reveal treasure and catch thieves by invoking spirits, fallen angels, demons and faeries.

Including a conjuration said to have been performed at the request of Edward IV, King of England.

Being a partial transcription of Sloane MS 3824

WITH INTRODUCTION & COMMENTARY BY
DAVID RANKINE

PUBLISHED BY AVALONIA

Published by Avalonia

BM Avalonia
London
WC1N 3XX
England, UK

www.avaloniabooks.co.uk and www.avaloniabooks.com

THE BOOK OF TREASURE SPIRITS
With introduction and commentary by David RAnkine

ISBN-10: 1-905297-27-0
ISBN-13: 978-1-905297-27-6

First Edition, 7 September 2009

Design by Satori
Copyright © David Rankine and Avalonia 2009
Cover Image "Green Dragon" by Io Lig (c) 2009

British Library Cataloguing in Publication Data. A catalogue record for this book is available from the British Library

All rights reserved. No part of this publication may be reproduced or utilized in any form or by any means, electronic or mechanical, including photocopying, microfilm, recording, or by any information storage and retrieval system, or used in another book, without written permission from the authors.

THIS BOOK IS DEDICATED TO
SIR HANS SLOANE
(1660 – 1753)

ACKNOWLEDGEMENTS

I would like to thank the British Library for supplying the copy of Sloane MS 3824 for me to work with. I would like to thank Stephen Skinner, who continues to encourage me and provide many hours of interesting discussion on the subject close to our hearts that we write about together – the grimoires. I would also like to thank Dan Harms for drawing my attention to Folger MS Vb 26. Finally, my thanks and appreciation to my beautiful wife Sorita who is my personal treasure, providing me with sustenance and inspiration.

Contents

Introduction	11
About the Manuscript	19
Contents of Sloane MS 3824	22
SLOANE MS 3824	23
Prayer to call Spirits of Darkness	24
Invocation of Lucifer, Beelzebub & Sathan	27
An Operation for Obtaining Treasure Trove	30
The Invocation	32
A General Invocation	48
An Experiment to Cause a Thief to Return	55
The Prayer	58
The Consecrations & Benedictions	68
Experiment to call Spirits that Guard Treasure	84
Of Spirits and Fairies	94
Conjuration of Treasure Spirits	101
The Fairy Court and Treasure	108
Of Types of Treasure & Hauntings	115
Experiment to obtain Treasure Trove	120
Experiment with Bret	127
Conjuration of Birto for King Edward IV	131
Conjuration of Bealpharos	134
Of Evil Spirits	139

Experiment of Vassago	140
Experiment of Agares	145
An Experiment to Obtain Your Desire	153
Experiment of Bleth	156
Of the Demon Rulers	162
Appendix 1: The Spirit Contract for Padiel	174
Bibliography	176
Index	179

Introduction

In past centuries the British monarchy was well known for its interest in treasure, as seen by the licensing of explorers and buccaneers. However the royal interest in magic was discrete and largely unknown. When magic and treasure met, the crown became extremely interested. For centuries the reigning monarchs granted licences to nobles and well-to-do figures to search for treasure trove, in return for a percentage of the findings. In the period from 1237-1621 authorizations were given for treasure seeking in a number of counties, particularly those in the southern parts of England like Cornwall, Devon and Dorset.

For example, in 1521, King Henry VIII granted a licence to Sir Edward Belknap, John Hertford and John Jonys (a goldsmith) to dig in Cornwall and Devon for treasure.[1] As well as magicians and cunning-folk, priests were frequently called upon by treasure-seekers to raise spirits, as it was believed that such treasures were rarely unguarded. However records do also show that the fairy king Oberion refused to talk to them![2]

Licences may have been granted in some instances to control the actions of enterprising individuals who sought to make their fortunes illicitly through such quests for buried treasure. In a time before the stability of the banking system, people often buried their money, and had done for centuries since before the Romans. As a result of this the quest for treasure was a common one.

This made the ruins of fine buildings, such as castles, monasteries and stately homes particularly obvious targets. Likewise old burial mounds and sites were considered prime

---

[1] *On Treasure Trove and Invocation of Spirits*, Turner, 1846.
[2] *Ibid.*

candidates for buried treasure. As Grinsell observed, *"The motive for depositing coin-hoards in barrows (and other precisely pin-pointed ancient monuments) in Roman times must have been the need to conceal treasure during periods of unrest."*[3] The digging up of such sites for treasure was a common occurrence, to the extent that the term *'hill-digger'* was used for a person on the make. Another such term was *'cross-digger'*, due to the belief that stone crosses often marked treasure. The result of this was an ongoing tendency for such crosses to be pulled down by hopeful thieves, as shown by three men being charged at Chester in 1615 for pulling down stone crosses.

The search for treasure even extended to major buildings that were not ruined. In 1634 a treasure-hunting expedition was conducted in Westminster Abbey, led by the King's clock-master Davy Ramsey using Mosaical Rods,[4] with the blessing and encouragement of the Dean of the Abbey (in exchange for a percentage of any proceeds). Accompanying him were a number of others, including the famous astrologer William Lilly, who would later be tried for arson for having accurately predicted the Fire of London some years prior to its occurrence (he was found innocent of starting the fire!). Lilly's description of events is interesting, not least because it indicates guardian demon spirits in the Abbey! Lilly wrote:

> *"We played the hazel rod round about the cloister; upon the west side of the cloisters the rods moved one over another, an argument that the treasure was there. The labourers digged at least six feet deep and there we met with a coffin ... From the cloisters we went into the Abbey church, where, upon a sudden (there being no wind when we began), so fierce, so high, so blustering and loud a wind did rise, that we verily believed the west end of the church would have fallen upon us. Our rods would not move at all;*

---

[3] *Barrow Treasure in Fact, Tradition and Legislation,* Grinsell, 1967.
[4] A fancy name for hazel divining rods.

the candles and torches, all but one, were extinguished, or burned very dimly. John Scott, my partner, was amazed, looked pale, knew not what to think or do, until I gave directions and command to dismiss the demons; which, when done, all was quiet again."[5]

Lilly went on to comment that he put the failure down to the fact that the group comprised thirty or so people, many of whom were derisive. He declared that he believed the west side of the church would have probably been blown down if he had not dismissed the demons. His closing remark demonstrates a real appreciation of the best parameters for such work, when he declared:

"Secrecy and intelligent operators, with a strong confidence and knowledge of what they are doing, are best for this work."[6]

Another instance from the reign of King Henry VIII was recorded by the monk William Stapleton in 1528, where in the pursuit of treasure *"one Denys of Hofton did bring me a book called Thesaurus Spirituum*[7] *and, after that, another called Secreta Secretorum,*[8] *a little ring, a plate, a circle, and also a sword for the art of digging."*[9]

The reference to plates is interesting, as several of the conjurations in this manuscript use engraved plates as part of the equipment. William Stapleton mentioned a plate made for the calling of Oberion, who is also within this manuscript. The parallels are suggestive of the essential equipment used in the conjuration of spirits for locating treasure. It is also significant that Stapleton explained how after obtaining a license to seek treasure,

---

[5] *David Ramsay and the Diving Rod*, Timbs, 1865.
[6] *Ibid.*
[7] Another name for the *De Nigromancia* of Roger Bacon.
[8] A book of theurgic magic dealing almost exclusively with angels.
[9] *On Treasure Trove and Invocation of Spirits*, Turner, 1846.

he spoke again to Denys, who informed him he would bring him two cunning-men.

One of the most important politicians of the late seventeenth century was Goodwin Wharton (1653-1704) who may be seen as the Indiana Jones of his time, and who rose to become Lord Admiral of the British Fleet. Wharton was aided for many years by the ex-leveller John Wildman and a spirit (of an executed criminal) called George, and went on various treasure quests including one for the legendary Urim and Thummim, the twin jewels from the High Priest's Breastplate described in the Bible.

Keith Thomas described Wharton as spending the last twenty-five years of the seventeenth century being *"almost continuously engaged in a treasure quest for which he enlisted spirits, fairies and the latest resources of contemporary technology"*.[10] He even invented diving gear, allegedly with the aid of angels, in order to try and raise sunken treasure from a Spanish galleon off the north coast of Scotland.

The modern descendants of the quest for treasure trove exist in three forms. On the esoteric level there are psychic questers, people such as Andrew Collins and Graham Philips who use psychics to aid them in quests for buried magical objects. On the mundane level we see archaeologists, seeking to learn from the past, and treasure-seekers with their metal detectors, seeking to profit from the past.

This book contains all of the treasure-related conjurations and information from the material in Sloane MS 3824. The manuscript is a unique combination of material which seems to date to 1649, with some material being possibly earlier and some later, giving a range of 1641-59.

Probably the most startling reference in the manuscript is the one made to the English King, Edward IV (reigned 1461-83) in *"An Experiment of the Spirit Birto as hath often been proved at the instant request of Edward the Fourth King of England."* The long history of

---

[10] *Religion and the Decline of Magic*, Thomas, 1973.

interest in matters magical from the crown is now becoming more apparent, such as Queen Elizabeth I's association with Dr John Dee and discussions on alchemy and magic. Likewise the presence of grimoires such as *Liber Juratus* in the Royal Library cannot be entirely ignored.

This conjuration exists in an earlier form in Folger MS Vb 26, which dates to around 1580, some sixty years earlier, and this manuscript also includes reference to Oberion. Subsequent versions of this conjuration were reproduced by notable figures of the late eighteenth and nineteenth century, such as Frederick Hockley (Wellcome MS 3203) and Ebenezer Sibley (e.g. John Rylands GB 0133 Eng MS 40) as *"An Experiment of me J.W. with the Spirits Birto, Agares, Balphares & Vassago as hath often been proved at the instant request of Edward the Fourth King of England."* Whilst the inclusion of the Goetic spirits Agares and Vassago in the title is interesting, it is in derivative manuscripts nearly two hundred years after this manuscript (Sloane MS 3824), despite referring to content from this manuscript. That this should be a later addition is much more plausible, as there are no known manuscripts of the *Goetia* prior to 1641, the date of Sloane MS 3825, which is the earliest extant version.

One of the most unusual features of the conjuration is the requirement for an image of a dragon to be included in the practice. This may be derived from the idea of dragons as guardians of treasure trove, as seen in British literature from the eighth century classic *Beowulf* onwards.

Looking at the sources of the material in Sloane MS 3824, we must consider diverse sources. From the use of certain divine names and phrases in the conjurations, such as *'Archima Rabur'* and *'Aye Saraye'*, it is clear that the *Heptameron* was a primary source for some of the material. This might seem obvious when we consider the inclusion of chapters from the *Heptameron* and Agrippa's *De Occulta Philosophia* in the MSS. However, significantly these chapters are in English prior to the first publication of the works, as the MSS dates to 1649, and *De Occulta Philosophia* was first published in English in 1651, with the *Heptameron* being first published in English in 1655 by Robert Turner.

The translation is similar to Turner's, but with some notable differences. One obvious difference is that the earthen vessel in Turner's translation is given as copper in Sloane MS 3824. An interesting variation is that in Sloane MS 3824 the phrase *'company'* is used rather than *'servants'*, implying a very different approach in the group dynamic associated with the conjuring magician. Another difference is that conjurations left in Latin by Turner are translated into English in Sloane MS 3824.

The group factor is also seen in the conjurations gathered here in the repeated use of *'we'* rather than *'I'* in the conjurations, emphasising the group-based nature of the material.

A particularly noteworthy point is the use of the divine name *Madzilodarp* in the General Invocation. 'Mad-Zilodarp', is an Enochian term, found in the Sixteenth Key and meaning *"The God of Stretch Forth and Conquer"*. Not only does it indicate that the magician who created the invocation was familiar with the Enochian calls received by Dr John Dee in the 1580s, but it is also probably the earliest instance of an Enochian god-name being used outside the system as a word of power, pre-dating the rituals of the Golden Dawn by centuries.

Here we might again question dating, as the first publication of Dee's diary material with this divine name in was Meric Causabon's *True and Faithful Relation* in 1659. However, as this manuscript was part of a corpus which included some material derived from Dee's Enochian work, it is not impossible that the owner had seen the Enochian calls. That some of the material dates to 1659 or later is also possible and cannot be dismissed, giving a range from 1641-1659 for the material.

The strong influence of the *Goetia* is seen in the nine Goetic spirits who are mentioned in the context of conjurations for treasure. These are Agares, Andromalius, Asmodai, Barbatos (Barbaros), Bileth (Bleth), Dantalion, Gorson, Seere, and Vassago.

The spirit Alpherez is also mentioned, who is the Prince of the Second Chora in the *Art Almadel*.

The invocation of the spirit Bealpharos (Bealphares), and the accompanying images, were drawn from Reginald Scot's *Discoverie of Witchcraft* (1584), showing how this significant sixteenth century book, rather than serving its author's purpose of ridiculing magic, acted as a source of material for magicians.

The spirit Barbasan, who is described as a servant spirit to Baramper, seems, rather curiously, to be first mentioned in Shakespeare's play *The Merry Wives of Windsor*.[11] Clearly this name was known if Shakespeare quoted it, though I have not found reference in any earlier grimoires or texts to it.

Another indication of the late sixteenth century influence apart from the material drawn from Scot is the juxtaposition of Lucifer, Beelzebub and Sathan as the heads of the infernal hierarchies. These three spirits were linked by King James I of England (James VI of Scotland) in his work *Daemonologie* (1597). Although James I equated the three spirits to each other as being the same being, it was nevertheless in his work that they were first specifically drawn together as a triad. Earlier works such as the fifteenth century Munich CLM 849 had included all three of these spirits, but in lists with others, and not as a specific grouping.

Some of the conjurations in this text are echoed in the material found in the nineteenth century *Libellus Magicus*, or *Magical Book of the Jesuits*. This grimoire, which seems to date to 1845, is part of the Faustian tradition of material, and contains several conjurations and dismissals specifically aimed at dealing with treasure spirits, particularly focusing on treasures from the sea, which is also found in Sloane MS 3824.

Other grimoires and early texts which include material focused on locating treasure are the fifteen century *Abramelin*, and the sixteenth century *Archidoxes of Magic* (by Paracelsus), and *Key*

---

[11] *"I am not Barbason, you cannot conjure me", The Merry Wives of Windsor*, Shakespeare

of Solomon.[12] Of these, Paracelsus concentrated on describing phenomena surrounding possible treasure locations and declared that the guardians were usually pygmies (earth elementals) or sylphs (air elementals). The *Abramelin* has a chapter with different magic squares to be used for retrieving all different types of treasure, and the *Key of Solomon* includes magical pentacles which can be used for the obtaining of treasure.

The eighteenth century *Sixth and Seventh Books of Moses* also includes seals for finding treasure, with one which is said to bring treasure to the surface if it is buried in the location! The early nineteenth century works the *Black Pullet* and the *Grimorium Verum* both included details of how to find treasure, be it through magical rings or using coins and the wand.

The type of treasure being sought was described in wide-ranging terms, as would be expected when dealing with spirits, to ensure that all options were covered. Thus the magician requested treasure *"of Gold & Silver, Coin, Plate, Bullion, Jewels, or other Goods and Chattels"*. In the same vein, there are three spirit contracts in this manuscript, to the spirits Agares and Vassago in respect of treasure trove conjurations, and also to the spirit Padiel (included as Appendix 1 for completion), making this the largest single grouping of such contracts to my knowledge.

It is interesting that the author should acknowledge in the text that the style of the conjurations was *"Long in the effecting, and bringing thereof to pass, and to be a piece of tedious & tiresome practice"*. Nowhere else in the grimoires is such a blatant declaration of the labour-intensive practice of conjuration made in this manner. Now, as then, it is up to the practitioner to decide whether they wish to invest the time and energy into such practices.

David Rankine
Powys, June 2009

---

[12] See *The Veritable Key of Solomon*, Skinner & Rankine, 2008.

About the Manuscript

Although it might seem somewhat muddled, the internal detail of the manuscript makes its position within the grimoire tradition more clear. On folio 4, at the top of the page, is a large letter 'L', which continues a sequence seen in Sloane MS 3825. Sloane MS 3825 is a manuscript which combines three distinct works. The first part, which also has letter headings (ending in 'K'), is the *Janua Magica Reserata* (*'Keys to the Gateway of Magic'*). Following this is the *Nine Keys* of Dr Thomas Rudd,[13] and the third part, in a different hand, is the earliest extant edition of the *Lemegeton*.[14]

Much of the material in *Janua Magica Reserata* refers to or contextualises material found in Sloane MS 3824, which was clearly originally bound with it. Both Sloane MS 3824 and MS 3825 were purchased by Sir Hans Sloane in 1740 from the sale of Sir Joseph Jekyll's manuscripts, as was Sloane MS 3821. These manuscripts contained material regarding the Planetary Intelligences which ended mid-conjuration in Sloane MS 3825 but may be found in its entirety in Sloane MS 3821, emphasising the interconnectedness of these manuscripts.

Further evidence of the interconnectedness of these manuscripts may be seen in the identical style of the conjurations, of Enochian spirits, demon princes, demons, archangels and planetary intelligences. This then provides a corpus of material which was probably worked as a single body of work, and contained:

---

[13] The first two parts are reproduced in *The Keys to the Gateway of Magic*, Skinner & Rankine, 2005.
[14] Reproduced in *The Lesser Key of Solomon*, Peterson, 2001.

MSS	Conjurations
Sloane 3821	Enochian Hierarchies of Spiritual Creatures Demon Kings of the Directions Planetary Intelligences
Sloane 3824	Demon Rulers (Lucifer, Beelzebub & Sathan) Goetic Spirits for Treasure Treasure Spirits Demons of Trithemius' *Steganographia* (incomplete)
Sloane 3825	Nine Archangels Planetary Intelligences (incomplete) Goetic Spirits (including rest of *Lemegeton* spirits)

The *Pauline Art* (part three of the *Lemegeton* in Sloane MS 3825) refers to a date of 1641, giving an age for this manuscript which is consistent with the style of the handwriting. However material in Sloane MS 3824 written by Elias Ashmole can be dated to 1649. This suggests that the material was added together as a collection over a period of time, as would be expected.

The provenance of the manuscripts, passing from Baron John Somers (1651-1716), Lord Chancellor of England, to his brother-in-law Sir Joseph Jekyll (1663-1738), Master of the Rolls, to Sir Hans Sloane (1660-1753), demonstrates the involvement of peers at the highest level of British government, so the idea that a conjuration should be performed for a monarch is not as extraordinary as it might otherwise seem. From Sir Hans Sloane, the manuscripts were all left to the British Museum (now the British Library) as part of what has become known as the Sloane collection.

I have included the material from folios 3-21b, and 91-122b, as being all of that relating to treasure spirits, which is not found elsewhere. Much of the other material is early translations of other material which may be found in other books, such as the extracts from the *Heptameron* (included to show differences and for its practical value), Agrippa's *Occult Philosophy* (not included) and part of Book 1 of Trithemius' *Steganographia* (under the name *Trithemius Redivivus*). The part of the *Steganographia* is to my knowledge the first English (part-)translation done of this work, dating as it does to the mid-seventeenth century.

It should be noted that the section headings have been added into the text for clarity and were not part of the original manuscript. Additionally the illustrations have all been redrawn, faithfully to the originals, to ensure clarity of the images, which in some instances were faded. Where a word is in bold as a sub-heading, it was emboldened in the original, whereas any bold word in the text was written in red in the original manuscript. Although the punctuation may seem erratic, with missing full stops and curious commas, it has been faithfully reproduced from the original. In the footnotes, the following abbreviations are used:

S: Sloane MS 3825
T: Turner's translation of the Heptameron

Contents of Sloane MS 3824

Folio	Content
3-5	A Prayer to be said before the calling forth of Elemental or Infernal Powers, or Spirits of Darkness
5b-13	An Operation for the obtaining of Treasure Trove using the Goetic spirits
13b-15b	A General Invocation, Conjuration or Constringation, moving and calling forth, any particular Aerial, Terrestrial, or other Elemental or Infernal, or other wandering Spirit or Spirits
16-21b	An excellent & approved Experiment, to cause a Thief to come again with the Goods he hath stolen; & to cause any Fugitive to return again.
22-28b	Extract from the Heptameron of Peter de Abano[15]
29-52b	Extract from Cornelius Agrippa's Occult Philosophy (not included)[16]
53-78b	The Second part of the Art of King Solomon (not included)[17]
79-90b	Circuli, figurae varia of Sigilla image magica (not included), includes The Tenth Key[18]
91-122b	An Experiment to Call out Spirits that are Keepers of Treasure Trove
123-132b	Trithemius Redivivus (not included)[19]
133-154b	The Magick and magical Elements of the 7 days of the week with their Appropriate Houses and the 4 annual Seasons[20] (not included)

---

[15] Reproduced in *The Fourth Book of Occult Philosophy*, Agrippa, 2004

[16] Reproduced in *Three Books of Occult Philosophy*, Agrippa, 1992.

[17] Reproduced in *The Goetia of Dr Rudd*, Skinner & Rankine, 2007.

[18] Reproduced in *The Keys to the Gateway of Magic*, Skinner & Rankine, 2005.

[19] An extract of Book 1 of the *Steganographia*, which is reproduced in *The Steganographia of Johannes Trithemius*, Mclean, 1982.

[20] Reproduced in *The Fourth Book of Occult Philosophy*, Agrippa, 2004.

SLOANE MS 3824

Prayer to call Spirits of Darkness

A Prayer to be said before the calling forth of Elemental or Infernal Powers, or Spirits of Darkness.

O most high, Immense, Immortal, Incomprehensible, and Omnipotent Lord God of Hosts, the only Creator of Heaven & Earth, & of all things contained therein; who, amongst all other admirable works of the Creation, hast made Man, according to the express Image of thy self, dignifying him with more divine, Celestial & Sublime Excellency, & superior part and participation, cohering with the most high & sacred Godhead, Angels, Heavens, Elements, & Elemental things, & given him an Imperial Sovereignty, over all Sublunar things in the Creation, both Animal, Vegetable, Mineral & Elemental: and next even to thy self under the Heavens, as a benefit and prerogative proper only to Man, & to no other Creature: And who hath likewise given to Man, a Sovereign power over all sublunar Spirits, both Aerial, Terrestrial & otherwise Elemental, residing in Orders & Mansions proper, & other wandering Spirits out of Orders or Mansions proper, both of Light & Darkness, & also Infernal Spirits, & subjected them to his Obedience & Service, whensoever he shall Command, Constrain, Call forth & move them to visible appearance, in order thereunto.

Now then O most high & heavenly God we thy humble Servants, reverently here present in thy holy fear, do beseech thee in thine infinite Mercy & paternal goodness, that all

Sublunar Spirits both Elemental and residing in Orders, & otherwise wandering out of Orders, both of Light & Darkness, & also Infernal Powers, may at the reading & rehearsal of our Invocations, Conjurations & Constraingacons,[21] & by thee commanded, & compelled, & constrained, obediently and peaceably to move & appear visibly, in fair & decent Form: & Shape, & in no wise hurtful, dreadful, terrible or affrightful, or otherwise in any violence or violent manner unto us, & here before us in these Glass Receptacles, or otherwise, to appear out of them here before us, in like serene, fair & decent manner, as shall be most convenient & necessary for any action, thing or matter, that they are called for to such appearances; & to serve & obey us, & to fulfil & go forth in our will, desires & Commandments in all & every several & particular matters & things respectively, wherein their Office & Orders are concerned, or whereunto in any wise they properly appertain;

& also to depart from our presence, & obediently & peaceably to return to their Orders & Places of residence, when they have conformed & fulfilled all our Will and Commandments; And that we shall discharge them for the time present, & time future; or shall accordingly give them Licence so to do, and also to be ready from time to time at our Call, & at all times to appear visibly unto us, & to serve & obey us, & to fulfil all our requests whatsoever we shall command them, & also to return to their Orders in peace, when we shall give them Licence to depart thereunto, without violence, injury, harm, prejudice or other mischief or mischievous matter to be done unto us or this Place, or to any other person or places whatsoever. Amen.

---

[21] Constraints.

The Lord bless us & keep us, the Lord make his Face shine upon us, & be gracious unto us: the Lord lift up his Countenance upon us, & give us his Peace.

Invocation of Lucifer, Beelzebub & Sathan

[22]O All you Spirits of great power **Lucifer Beelzebub Sathan**[23] unto whom By Orders & Offices, as Messengers of wrath,& Ministers of divine Justice, the Execution of God's Judgements are committed, & accordingly at his Commandment by you fulfilled, on all sublunar things, Creatures & places whatsoever & wheresoever he shall decree and appoint the same to be inflicted: And otherwise also & against sundry & many other times, preordained you by Orders & Offices, to serve & assist the Sons of men, living upon Earth, Servants of the most high God, whensoever you shall be invoked, moved, requested, commanded & constrained thereunto:

Now therefore know ye; O all ye Spirits **Lucifer Beelzebub Sathan** that we, Servants of the most high God, reverently here present in his holy fear, being dignified in this holy Trinity, with celestial power & authority, given to Man at his Creation, & to his successive posterity & Generations, unto the utmost period of time, above & over all Sublunar Spirits, of all Degrees, Natures, Orders & Offices, both Aerial, Terrestrial & otherwise Elemental, or wandering out of Orders, or Infernal, whether of Light or Darkness, from the Superior to

---

[22] A large capital L: heads this page above the prayer.
[23] This is contracted to *"L: B: S:"* in the manuscript, but clearly refers to these three Spirits, as later conjurations demonstrate.

the Inferior; do by the Name of your God, & by your Seals & Characters, most firmly & solidly subjecting & binding you by Orders & Office, both to the divine command of the highest & his Servants the Sons of Men, now living on Earth:

We do Exorcise, Conjure, Command, Constrain & move you, O all you Spirits **Lucifer Beelzebub Sathan** to subject all Spirits whatsoever, from the Superior to the Inferior, that have place & Residence in any, or all, & every of your several & respective Orders or Mansions, or that shall otherwise under your power, government & Command unto us, & our Invocations, Conjurations & Constringations.

And that whensoever & wheresoever we shall at any time, & in any place, Conjure, Command, Constrain, Call forth & move them, by Names, Orders & Offices, or any or either of them, that then & there, even at any every instant time, be enforced, compelled & constrained to move & appear, in fair & decent forms, & in no wise hurtful, dreadful, terrible or affrightful unto us, or this place, or to any other person or place whatsoever, but in all humility & serenity, visibly to the sight of our Eyes, either in these Glass Receptacles[24] or any of them standing here before us, for that purpose, according to a usual way of receiving & enclosing Spirits at their appearance, Or otherwise out of them here before us, according as best befitteth, or shall be most beneficial & convenient for us, in all or any such our Operations & Affairs, as the necessity or occasion thereof shall require.

And to show forth unto us true & visible signs, foregoing their coming & appearance. And to make true & faithful Answers unto us, & also to reveal, discover & show forth unto us, the very truth & certainty of all such our purposeful

---

[24] Contracted to *"G:R:"*, this is a common contraction.

matters & things in question, & to fulfil, perform & accomplish unto us, all these our demands & Requests, as lyeth here before us.[25] *And also furthermore, as in the content of our Invocations, Conjurations & Constringations, shall more fully & at large be declared & expressly rehearsed: speaking plainly unto us, so as that we may both hear & understand them.*

All which as aforesaid, we do powerfully Exorcise, Conjure, Command, Compel Constrain & move you, O all you Spirits **Lucifer Beelzebub Sathan** *in the Name of your God, & by the Seals of your Orders, preordinately decreed of the most high God, confirming, Subjecting and binding you by Orders & Office, into strict Obedience; first to the fulfilling of his Divine Will & pleasure, both at his instant & immediate Commandments & Appointments, And secondly as well unto the Service, Obedience & Assistance of his Servants the Sons of Men, now living on Earth, in your several & respective Orders & Offices, as to seduce, subvert & seek to destroy them by your evil Temptations, or any other wicked, subtle, crafty insinuations & illusions: And by the Celestial power of the most high & holy Trinity, wherewith we are now through divine Grace, dignified, armed & supported, to do, fulfil, perform & accomplish for & unto us, both now at this time present, & also at all other times, whensoever we shall move, request & command them thereunto, without delay delusion or disturbance, whereby to surprise or assault our senses with fears & amazements: or in any wise to obstruct or hinder the effects of these our present Operations, by any subtle Craft or illusions whatsoever, &c.*

---

[25] This implies a list of requests made by the magician to ensure nothing is forgotten in the heat of ritual.

An Operation for Obtaining Treasure Trove

An Operation for the obtaining of Treasure Trove; The Key whereof is hidden, from some principal Spirit, who may be Invocated or Called forth by Name, Nature, Degree, Order & Office for that purpose, by the content of the following Invocation; the foregoing Prayer & Conjuration being obliged to be first used or said; which Rule ought also to be remembered before Invocation is made, for any Infernal Spirits or powers of Darkness.

A Select Invocation, moving & calling forth some certain Spirits, who by Names are called **Sulpher**,[26] &c: and who are said by Nature, degree, Order & Office, not only to have the keeping & possession of many & several Treasures or Treasuries of Gold & Silver, both in Coin, Plate, Gems, Bullion, & other goods & Chattels of considerable value, that hath been manufactured, & in use among the Sons of Men, & said to be corrupted of them. And both heretofore of ancient, & by them of later times, either through Envy or Necessity, or otherwise by chance, purpose or appointment of them conceived, & kept from the knowledge, use & benefit of Posterity.

But also doth well know, how otherwise, by what Spirit, any such Treasures or Treasuries shall be kept or possessed,

---

[26] This name may be drawn from alchemy, as it does not seem to occur in any of the other grimoires.

be they of what name, nature, degree, order & Offices soever. And who also by Office hath power given them, to discharge or dismiss and call forth, any such Spirit so keeping any such Treasures or Treasuries, and constrain them to deliver and yield up, & to bring the same wheresoever it shall be appointed &c.

The Invocation

O all ye Spirits, who have power given you to visit the parts of the Earth, & to execute the Commandments of the highest, and also by divine permission, to appear unto the Sons of Men, Servants of the most high God, living on Earth, whensoever they shall Invoke & call you forth to visible appearance, to obey them, to serve them, & to be friendly unto them, at such their Calls & Invocations made unto you, & readily forthwith to fulfil & perform all such their Commandments & requisite, wherein your Offices are properly & pertinently concerned, or in any wise appertaining.

And accordingly unto such their addresses & invocations as are made, & by your Offices given & referred unto you, O all ye Spirits of great power in the keeping of hidden Treasuries, & also of the hiding, discovering & yielding up the same to the Sons of Men for whose use it was principally & primarily decreed & ordained: We do exorcise, call upon & Conjure you, O all you Spirits, jointly & severally by Names, Orders & Offices, who are known unto the Sons of Men, from the Tradition of their predecessors, by the names of **Sulphur, Chalcos,**[27] **Anaboth,**[28] **Sonenel, Barbaros, Gorson,** (or **Gorzon) Everges, Mureril, Vassago, Agares, Baramper,**

---

[27] Chalcos is the Greek for *'Copper'*, which would continue the alchemical theme in names.

[28] Annabath is one of the spirits in Folger MS Vb 26, and considering the similarity of the names, is probably the source of Anaboth. I have not seen all of the MS at this stage, and so cannot comment if other names are also found there.

Barbasan, *of what nature soever you are, whether wandering Spirits, or Aerial or Terrestrial, or otherwise Elemental or Infernal powers, applying either to Light or darkness or both, in the most true & special Name of your God, and by the force, influence, power & virtue thereof, & by all the power both divine, Celestial & Terrestrial, the most high God hath given both to Angels & to Men, & by your seals & Characters, most firmly & solidly binding, subjecting and obliging you by Orders & Offices, both the divine commands of the highest, & his servants the sons of Men, calling forth & moving you thereunto.*

By all aforesaid we do again Exorcise, Call upon, Conjure, Command & Constrain all you Spirits By Name **Sulphur**, **[Chalcos]**,[29] **Anaboth**, **Sonenel**, **Barbaros**, **Gorson**, *(or* **Gorzon***)* **Everges**, **Mureril**, **Vassago**, **Agares**, **Baramper**, **Barbason**, *and all other by Office, having power given to them to range and orbit the Earth, & all parts thereof, and to possess & keep, not only the natural Mines of Gold & Silver, but also many other Treasures, both in Coin, Plate & Bullion, or Jewels of great value, or any other goods or Chattels, that has been the Manufacturison*[30] *of Men, & heretofore in use among them, buried in the Earth, or otherwise laid up & hidden, in some very secret place or places therein, And so thereby said to be corrupted of them & amongst them, whereby Posterity is denied, the benefit of, & comfort thereof:*

Wherefore divine Justice hath given such powers, whether Aerial, Terrestrial or otherwise Elemental or Infernal;

---

[29] This name was omitted here in the original, though this was obviously a copyist's error.

[30] I.e. manufactured.

or other wandering Spirits, both of Light & darkness, & conversant in all Elemental parts & places, Mediums or Messengers, executing the Judgements of the Highest, at his Omnipotent, both mediate & immediate Commandments: and taking arrogance[31] on the Sins & Offences & causes thereof, acted and committed by the Ancestors or Predecessors of the Sons of Men: both heretofore of old, & thence of late times, not only upon them, but also many other successive Generations; even to the utmost period of time (as in the mind, Will & pleasure of the all powerful, is preordinately decreed) whose divine Grace & Mercy defendeth at the humble Supplications Petitions & Addresses of his servants the Sons of Men, to their assistance, in obtaining and recovering all such Treasures & Treasuries, so buried, laid up, or otherwise secretly hidden, either in or upon the Earth, whither of old or of later times, for what cause or intent soever the same was buried, hidden or otherwise concealed, & still at this time kept from the knowledge, understanding, use, benefit & comfort of Men, dignifying & giving them full power & authority, both Celestial & Terrestrial, to Conjure, Command, Constrain, Call forth & move you, O all you Spirits forenamed & mentioned by Orders & Offices as aforesaid, both unto visible appearance; & also to serve them, & to obey them, & to fulfil & perform all such their Commandments, whatsoever they shall enjoin & command you, as according to your Orders & Offices, you are in the Name of the highest & heavenly, Conjured Compelled & Constrained to Obedience.

Now therefore know you, O all you Spirits by Name **Sulphur, Chalcos, Anaboth, Sonenel, Barbaros, Gorson,**

---

[31] The word is unclear in the original, however this is the most likely interpretation.

*(or **Gorzon**) **Everges, Mureril, Vassago, Agares, Baramper, Barbason**, and all other you Spirits, who by Orders & Office, have power & garrison given you, to possess & keep all such Treasures & Treasuries of Gold & Silver, Coin, Plate, Bullion, Jewels, or other Goods and Chattels, heretofore, in frequent & familiar use, & concealed amongst Men, & at this time lyeth buried, hidden or otherwise concealed in some secret place or places, in the Earth, or upon the Earth, (as aforesaid) that are the Servants of the most high God, and humbly present here at this time, in his holy fear, being assisted, supported, fortified & strengthened, by his all powerful Name, & being dignified by the power of his holy Spirit, with Celestial & Terrestrial perfection, as to the more supreme and primitive Idea, Angelical excellency, Imperial power, Sovereign authority and superior parts & participations, Cohering with the sacred Godhead, Angels, Heavens, Elements & Elemental things, surpassing all sublunary Creatures in the Creation, by the virtue & influence whereof, we being entrusted with pious sufficiency, have power given us thereby, over all Spirits, both Aerial, Terrestrial & otherwise Elemental or Infernal, of all Orders & Offices, to serve us & fulfil our Commands & Requests, whensoever we shall move & call them forth, in order thereunto, do Conjure, Command, Compel & Constrain; Call forth & move you, O all you Spirits aforesaid, or some one or any or more of you, jointly & severally, to appear visibly, in fair & decent form and in no wise turbulent, Terrible or Affrightful, or in any violent manner, or in any wise doing harm, unto us or this place, or to any other persons or places whatsoever (but we say) come ye in all Serenity, Affability & grace, & appear unto us in these Glass Receptacles or in any or all of them set here before us, for that purpose, or otherwise appear out of them visibly here before us, to the sight of our*

Eyes, according as it shall be convenient or best befitting this present Occasion, purpose or matter, & show forth visibly & plainly unto us, a foregoing sign or Sight of your appearance; for the which we now Conjure, move & call you forth, to reveal & show forth plainly unto us, & to Act, Do & perform for us in this present Operation & affair, as we shall propose request & make known unto you whensoever.

 O all you Spirits By Name **Sulphur, Chalcos, Anaboth, Sonenel,**[32] **Barbaros, Gorson,** (or **Gorzon**) **Everges, Mureril, Vassago, Agares, Baramper, Barbason**, hearken you unto this present, and unto this present Conjuration, Invocation & constriction, by the efficacy, virtue, power & force whereof, we do again Conjure, Command, Compel, & Constrain you all, or some one, or any, or more of you Spirits aforesaid, jointly & severally, to appear plainly here before us in these Glass Receptacles or otherwise out of them, visibly to the sight of our Eyes, or else that the Spirits called **Barbaros, Gorson, Everges, Mureril** & **Vassago**, or any one or more of them, or any other Spirit or Spirits, having power given unto them by orders or Office, or otherwise by divine Justice, pleasure & permission, to possess, detain & keep any Treasures or Treasuries, that are buried & hidden, or in any wise concealed from the knowledge use or benefit of Mankind, or kept from them by any Spirit or Spirits, of what Name, Order, or Office soever they are, or for what cause soever they do possess & keep the same, from the use of Mankind (as aforesaid) to reveal, discover, show forth & plainly make appear unto us the very truth & certainty thereof and what Spirit & Spirits by name & Orders, doth possess & keep the

---

[32] This name was recorded here as *Soninil* in the original MS, but I have corrected it for consistency.

same, whereby we may accordingly, Conjure, Compel & constrain them, or otherwise by this your assistance to enforce them, quietly, peaceably & willingly, without any turbulence or noise, to direct yield up & bring the same hither unto this place, or unto any other place whensoever we shall appoint, and here or there to leave the same, visibly & openly naked unto us, so that we may take & bear the same away for our necessary use,

& we do again yet further by those present, & the efficacy, power & force thereof, Conjure, Command, Compel & constrain you all ye Spirits by name (as aforesaid) **Sulphur**, **Chalcos**, **Anaboth**, **Sonenel**, **Barbaros**, **Gorson**, (or **Gorzon**) **Everges**, **Mureril**, **Vassago**, **Agares**, **Baramper**, **Barbasan**, or some one, or any, or more of you, jointly & severally, to appear visibly, meekly & peaceably, in decent forms before us, in these Glass Receptacles or otherwise out of them (as aforesaid) or to cause, compel & constrain a certain Spirit to appear visibly unto us in these Glass Receptacles or otherwise out of them here before us, in all serenity & peace, & in decent forms (as aforesaid) who is called **Camret**, & said to be a duke, or Spirit of great power & strength, & useful in serving the Sons of Men, by Orders and Office, in these operations & affairs, to reveal, discover, and show forth & make appear unto them, the very truth & certainty of any Treasure or Treasuries that is concealed, buried or hidden in or upon the Earth, And if any spirit or Spirits, of what Name, nature, Order or Office soever they are, doth possess & keep the same from the knowledge, use & benefit of Man, that he the said Spirit called **Camret**, may likewise Command, Compel & Constrain the said Spirits or keepers of any such Treasure, to admit, yield up & bring the same away unto such place or places wherefore it shall be appointed.

  And we do also yet further & again Exorcise, Conjure, Command, Compel, Constrain & powerfully move you, by the efficacy & force of this our Invocation, & the Celestial power & authority, by divine Grace wherewith we are dignified, O all ye Spirits by Name (as aforesaid) **Sulphur, Chalcos, Anaboth, Sonenel, Barbaros, Gorson,** (or **Gorzon**) **Everges, Mureril, Vassago, Agares, Baramper, Barbason**, that some one, or any or more, or all of you, with all power & force you have, or that is given unto you, at the Will & pleasure of the highest, you do command compel & constrain, those Spirits who are called by name **Scor** (or **Scarus**) **Roab, Zaym, Umbra**,[33] **Gijel**, or some one, or any, or more, or all of them, jointly or severally, in general & particular; who are said by nature, Order or Offices, to direct & call forth any Spirit or Spirits, that have the keeping of any such Treasures or Treasuries, hidden or buried in the Earth, or otherwise laid up or concealed, & so kept from the knowledge, benefit, use & comfort of the Sons of Men,

  & who also by Office, hath power to bring, or cause the same to be brought unto any place or places, wheresoever they shall be appointed to appear visibly, in fair & decent form unto us, in these Glass Receptacles or otherwise out of them here before us, & to show forth plainly unto us, visibly, a foregoing sign or Sight of their appearance, and to reveal the very truth & certainty of all such Treasures or Treasuries, as we shall propose unto them, & request of them, & to bring or cause the same to be brought unto us at any time or times, & in any such place or places, whensoever & wheresoever we shall then & there command & appoint them, And more specially & in particular, to discover such Treasures &

---

[33] As Umbra is Latin for *'shadow'*, this is probably the source of this name.

Treasuries, now by us proposed & in question, lying buried, or being otherwise hidden, and by certain report & credible information we believe & suppose in &c.

*And also to reveal & make known unto us, such Treasures & Treasuries, as are unknown; & so not in question, until a more full discovery by such your Information, or otherwise shall be made or given, of what Treasure soever is where in any wise, or in any place within the Realm of England, so called, hidden or buried, & so kept or concealed, from the knowledge use & benefit of Mankind, & to bring or cause the same to be brought unto this place, or to any other place where we shall appoint. Now then finally know you, O all ye Spirits by Name, Order & Office (as aforesaid) **Sulphur**, **Chalcos**, **Anaboth**, **Sonenel**, **Barbaros**, **Gorson**, (or **Gorzon**) **Everges**, **Mureril**, **Vassago**, **Agares**, **Baramper**, **Barbason**, that we do powerfully & confidently, Conjure, Command, Constrain, Call forth & move you to come away forthwith & immediately & at this our Invocation, without any further illusion or delay, & tarry not, neither defer the time of your coming one minute longer, but come presently away, from the place or places of your present residence, wheresoever you are, & appear you readily, willingly courteously, affably peaceably, plainly, visibly unto us, in fair & decent forms in these Glass Receptacles or otherwise out of them here before us;*

*Or else command, enforce & send unto us your Spirit called **Camret** or else move & send immediately at this our Call, some one, or any, or more of these Spirits, by name called **Scor** (or **Scarus**) **Roab**, **Zaym**, **Umbra**, & **Gijel**, to appear visibly unto us, in these Glass Receptacles or otherwise out of them, and plainly to show forth unto us, a foregoing sign: or Test of their appearance; & to give us true &*

faithful Answers, of all such questions, as we shall make demand of, & positively to answer us the very truth & certainty, of all such Treasures & Treasuries, of Gold & Silver, either in Coin, Plate, Bullion or Jewels, or any other Goods & Chattels, as are hidden buried or concealed in the Earth, or upon the Earth, in any place or places, Country or Countries, by what names soever called, or in what part or point of the Compass, or Angle of the Earth soever, bearing from this place, the same shall at this time continue in, hidden, buried or concealed from the knowledge, benefit, use or relief of mankind, whether it be kept by any Spirit or Spirits, of what Name, Nature, Order or Office soever they are; Or by any artificial or magical Charms, or by any envious or malignant crafts or subtleties, either of Elemental Terrestrial or Infernal Spirits, or of any wandering Spirits out of Orders, as by the traditions of Man as rationally supposed, & so credibly reported unto posterity, & by good testimony thereof is verily believed of us, to be accustomary & usual for all such Treasures so hidden, or by the long continuance of time, quite worn out of all knowledge & remembrances of Mankind, & so remaining in utter oblivion & forgetfulness as how or by what means so ever else, any such hidden Treasures is kept, or may be kept by Chance, purpose or appointment, or by nature simply through mortality, become wholly unknown to any living person, or so lyeth concealed from the understanding of posterity;

And that by either you, O all ye Spirits **Sulphur**, **Chalcos**, **Anaboth**, **Sonenel**, **Barbaros**, **Gorson**, *(or* **Gorzon**) **Everges**, **Mureril**, **Vassago**, **Agares**, **Baramper**, **Barbason**, *or any one, or other, or more of you, jointly & severally (as aforesaid) or by the Spirit* **Camret**, *or by all or many or more of these Spirits called* **Scor** *(or* **Scarus**) **Roab**, **Zaym**, **Umbra**,

Gijel, *or by whomsoever, or whatsoever spirit or power else, you shall send or cause to be sent, or come unto us, may not only appear here before us in these Glass Receptacles or otherwise out of them, & to show too a preceding Sign thereof (as aforesaid:) but also readily, willingly & obediently to serve us, in whatsoever we shall request & Command them, And immediately forthwith at such our command to fly & haste away, unto all or any such place or places, County or Countries, Town or Towns, House or Houses, Ground or Grounds, Cellars, Vaults, Caves, Nests, Ponds, Lakes, or any ruinous place, whatsoever any treasures are supposed to be hidden, buried or otherwise concealed from the knowledge of Man (as aforesaid) and to dismiss, cast out & discharge & send away, any or all such Spirit or Spirits (if any be there) that shall possess & keep any such Treasures or Treasuries, so hidden, buried & Concealed (as aforesaid:) And that either, or any, or some one or more of you, O all ye Spirits by name (as aforesaid) do bring or cause to be brought, either by your self or selves, or else that you compel & constrain the Spirit or Spirits, that doth possess & keep such hidden Treasure or Treasuries, to bring & bear away the same hither unto this place, &c: and here to leave the same with us, & to yield the same up unto us, & to our use, benefit & behoof, as in our own use & proper possession & claim, & then by virtue & power of our Commands accordingly, the said Spirit & Spirits, bearing & bringing away such Treasures or Treasuries unto us, may be dismissed & discharged therefrom, & of us enforced, at our Licence announced, & given them to depart away peaceably, in all mildness, meekness & serenity unto their Orders, or place of Residence, otherwise appointed for them: Notwithstanding any thing, matter, cause, craft,* subtlety, illusion dispute or other device or pretence to the contrary whatsoever.

 Finally & again, we do by these present, & by the virtue, power, influence, efficacy & force thereof, Conjure, Command, Compel, Constrain, and move you, O all you Spirits by name called **Sulphur**, **Chalcos**, **Anaboth**, **Sonenel**, **Barbaros**, **Gorson**, (or **Gorzon**) **Everges**, **Mureril**, **Vassago**, **Agares**, **Baramper**, **Barbason**, or any one or more or all of you, jointly and severally to appear unto us in these Glass Receptacles or otherwise out of them visibly here before us, & to compel & to constrain the Spirit called **Camret** to come immediately forthwith away accordingly, & visibly unto us (as aforesaid) or else to enforce & send immediately away unto us, any one or more of all of those Spirits called **Scor** (or **Scarus**) **Roab**, **Zaym**, **Umbra**, **Gijel**, to appear also accordingly & visibly unto us (as aforesaid) without Noise, Turbulence, Injury or violence, & in no way Terrible or affrightful to dismay or delude us, but to come or to send any other such Spirit unto us (as aforesaid) And to appear Obediently, peaceably, quietly, willingly, affably, readily & immediately here before us, in these Glass Receptacles or otherwise out of them (as aforesaid) & to show forth unto us ample, true, serene, affable & real signs & testimony of your & their coming & appearance, & to serve us in all these our Commands, as here before is mentioned;

 & not only to discover & bring or bear away hither unto us; or to any other place where soever we shall appoint, all such Treasures and Treasuries, as hath been at any time or times heretofore, buried, or hidden by our Ancestors, or Mankind then living on Earth, and at this time possessed or kept, by any Spirit or Spirits of what Element, Angle, Mansion, Order, Office, Name or nature soever, from the knowledge of &

benefit of Posterity or Mankind, now living on Earth, but to leave the same here present with us, or at any other such place, as we shall name & appoint, openly, nakedly, easily, plainly & visibly, to the sight of our Eyes, and So as that we may take, possess & carry away the same, as by & of right due & belonging unto us, & of our own proper Goods & Chattels, both of purchase & Inheritance,

And such Spirit or Spirits as possessed & kept, or that shall bring the same hither unto us, & that we shall have it in our full free assured & certain custody & possession, then afterwards immediately dismissed, discharged & sent away to their Orders or other places of abode, appointed them, they not daring or presuming to return, or offer to make any return to it again, either to carry the same away from us, or by any deceit or illusion, or other fraudulence seemingly to convert the same into any other vile or base matter, thing, form or Shape, otherwise than what it really is, or can be made appear to the contrary, and also to reveal discover, plainly show forth, & truly to make known, the very certain truth of all such Treasures & Treasuries that are laid up or hidden, either in the Earth, Caves, Cellars, Vaults, Houses, Ground, Pond, Lake, Well or old ruined Castle, monastery, ruinous Walls, or any other secret place whatsoever & whensoever, in any Angle, Country, City, Town; or Village, within this Realm or Kingdom of England, place, wherein we are now here present, that are not possessed, or kept by any Spirit or Spirits or otherwise, given them in Charge to keep & detain from the use & benefit of mankind, by any person or persons heretofore living on Earth, that you or some or any more of you, O all ye Spirits before named, may after a time & full discovery thereof is made known unto us, bring or cause to be brought hither unto us in this place, &c: all such Treasures & Treasuries, & to leave the same with us:

And so you Spirit or Spirits bringing or causing the same to be brought or conveyed hither, to give it up unto us, & then immediately to depart peaceably & quietly away, so as that we may take, enjoy, dispose, & convert the same unto our proper use & benefit, as of right belonging & appertaining unto us, without obtaining the similitude thereof in any wise, but to lay & leave the same barely open in its natural form & substance, as it was before the same was hidden, & as it is, and still may be & continue, Notwithstanding also the Craft or subtlety of any other Spirits, shall seemingly transform the same, or otherwise oppose or deceive us:

Or else, O all ye Spirits, or some one, or any, or more of you, as before we have called by Name, we do by these present, & by the virtue power & efficacy thereof; Conjure, Command, Compel & Constrain you to appear (as aforesaid) visibly unto us, either in these Glass Receptacles or otherwise out of them here before us, & to make known and apparently to show forth the very truth & certainty, of all such hidden Treasures & Treasuries, as we shall have in question, or make demand of, or otherwise request or Desire you, and to make true & faithful Answers, & give positive Results thereof unto us, & to inform, instruct & rightly direct us, how by all best, easiest, readiest & most assured ways or means, that can be contrived, found out or used, we may discover, find out & visibly see, & so perceive the same, so that by our industrious Labour and endeavours in our pursuit thereof, or by any other attempt, We shall make in pursuance thereof, We may both find out, obtain & take, & carry away the same, wheresoever we shall please, & possess enjoy & dispose thereof at our pleasure, as our own proper goods of right belonging unto us, And more especially & particular, all those, or any such Treasures or Treasuries, as for certain is reported, & as we are truly informed (& as we do, or may at least thereby verily believe to be true) that lyeth buried or otherwise hidden in *[34]* *[and by certain report & credible information we believe & suppose in &c.,] to show forth & make appear, the very truth & certainty thereof unto us, & either to bring, or cause the same to be brought hither to this place, or wheresoever else we shall appoint:*

And then such Spirit or Spirits, who shall bring & convey the same, according as we do command & appoint, may be immediately after they have laid down & left the same in place (accordingly as is appointed) dismissed discharged & compelled to depart away from it, & leaving the same barely & openly visible unto us, & so as that we may take & bear away the same, & also dispose thereof at pleasure, to our use & benefit, or else to inform & rightly direct us, how by all the best, easiest, & most assured ways, that can be conveniently and commodiously contrived & used, to find out, obtain, seize & carry away the same, & enjoy it to our use & benefit:

And to these our demands & requests, as we have now made, & as herein is contained & specified, we do by these present, & by virtue power & efficacy thereof, & in the name of the most high Omnipotent Lord God of Hosts, which all both Celestial, Terrestrial, Elemental Infernal, & other powers with fear & trembling, most reverently serve honour & obey, And by every & each of your several & respective Seals & Characters, most firmly & solidly binding, subjected &

---

[34] The text is marked with a * and a blank line following. From the style of the text it seems very likely the line added in square brackets is the appropriate one.

obliging you, by Orders & Offices, both to the divine command of the highest, & his servants the sons of Men, calling forth & moving you thereunto, Conjure, Command, Compel, Constrain, & move you, or some one, or any, or more of you, O all you Spirits by name called **Sulphur, Chalcos, Anaboth, Sonenel, Barbaros, Gorson,** *(or* **Gorzon)** **Everges, Mureril, Vassago, Agares, Baramper, Barbasan,** *& also* **Camret,** *& likewise* **Scor** *(or* **Scarus)** **Roab, Zaym, Umbra, Gijel,** *or any of them, to move & appear, in fair & decent form, visibly here before us, either in these Glass Receptacles or otherwise out of them, as the necessity & conveniency, of these our present occasions & affairs & as your service friendship & assistance, at these our calls & commands enjoined you therein, shall properly require:*

And appear you or some one or more of you, O all ye Spirits by name (as aforesaid) or send or cause to come and appear visibly unto us, some one or more Spirit or Spirits, who by Order & Office are alike, also qualified, readily & willingly to serve & assist us herein: Move (we say) & come immediately away meekly, obediently & peaceably & quietly, without Noise, or in any violent & turbulent manner, or in any wise affrightful terrible or dreadful, to assault or surprise our Senses or animal Spirits with fear or amazements, or doing any damage harm, injury or prejudice to us or to this place, or to any other place or persons whatsoever; but in all reverence, obedience & humility to appear, & make us true & perfect Answers, to all what we shall ask & demand, And effectually to fulfil & perform whatsoever we shall command, flying with haste away directly, unto such place & places wheresoever we shall send, & immediately with as much haste, to return back again to this place, or with as much speed as conveniently, can possibly afford or admit,

And to bring, or cause to be brought away hither to this place, all such Treasures or Treasuries, as are hidden or buried in the Earth, or otherwise laid & kept, from the knowledge use & benefit of mankind (as by certain report & credible information, is supposed & believed to lie hidden buried or otherwise concealed in *35 *[and we believe & suppose in &c.])*

And also any other such Treasures or Treasuries, as lie buried or hidden in the Earth, or otherwise in what place soever it is, not certainly known of us, & therefore not of us now simply proposed, singly mentioned, or had in particular question: Now then O all ye Spirits as before are mentioned or named, & all others not named, move then by Orders & Office proper; Move, come away, appear & plainly show forth, make known & reveal unto us, the very truth of all whatsoever we have hereby (as before is rehearsed) requested & demanded. And we do by these present and the power thereof, moreover Conjure, Compel & Constrain you O all ye Spirits by Name, Order & Office (as before specified,) in general & particular, jointly & severally, every & each one respectively, to serve & assist us herein, & effectually to fulfil & perform, all our Commandments to the very utmost; without further Apologies, excuse, penitence, hindrance, tarrying, delay, delusion, deceit, subtlety, craft, disguise, interruption, false motions, disturbances, fears, frights, amazements by any dreadful or terrible assault, or any other Illusions whatsoever, &c.

---

[35] The * in the original text obviously indicated a repetition of material, however it was not filled in by the copyist. From the text it seems likely that the line I have added in square brackets is the missing line.

A General Invocation

A General Invocation, Conjuration or Constringation, moving and calling forth, any particular Aerial, Terrestrial, or other Elemental or Infernal, or other wandering Spirit or Spirits, of what Name, Order, Office, Angle, Mansion, Nature, Degree or power whatsoever they are or may be of, or in any wise properly appertaining or belonging unto; which are to be mentioned in the following Invocation, whence the Letter **N:** is inserted, as being conveniently used thereunto, & so placed therein accordingly.

*O you Spirit, or Spiritual power, who is known of us from the Tradition of our Ancestors, & called by the Name **N:** of what nature Order, Office, Angle, Mansion or other place of abode wheresoever you are, or may be of, or do reside, frequent or in any wise properly or differently appertain or belong unto, or whether Elemental or Infernal, or other wandering Spirit or power, either of Light or darkness, having power given you to visit the Earth, & to execute the Commandments of the highest: and also by divine provision plainly & visibly, & in a fair & decent form to appear unto the Sons of Men, Servants of the most high God living on Earth, whensoever you shall be of them Invocated, Commanded, called forth, moved, & thereby Conjured, & constrained thereunto, to obey them, to serve them, & to be friendly unto them, & readily forthwith to fulfil & perform all such their commands & requests which they shall make; wherein by* nature Office order, place or power, you may in any wise be concerned or serviceable.

Know therefore O ye Spirit called by the Name **N:** (as aforesaid) that we the Servants of the most high God, & reverently here present in his holy fear, do Conjure, Command, Constrain, move & call you forth to visible Appearance, in the name of the most high **Madzilodarp**[36] and by the virtue and power of these his glorious, great, mighty & sacred Names, **Tetragrammaton, Jehovah, Adonay, Zebaoth,**[37] **Jah, Saday, Agla, El, Elohim, Alpha & Omega**, And who said, let us make Man, accordingly to our Image & Similitude, & let him bear rule over the works of our hands, & have sovereign power & command over all Sublunar Spirits, both Aerial, Terrestrial & otherwise Elemental, & other wandering Spirits & Infernal Spirits, of all Orders & offices whatsoever, both of Light & Darkness, & by your Seal & Character, most firmly & solidly binding, subjecting & obliging you by Order & Office, both to the divine Command of the Highest, & his servants the Sons of Men, calling forth & moving you thereunto.

And we do also further Conjure, Compel, Command, Constrain, Call forth & move you, By nature, degree, Order & Office, unto what Hierarchy Mansion or Place of residence whatsoever you appertain or belong unto, or wheresoever else you shall at this present be, either wandering out of Orders, or otherwise, O you Spirit, who is called **N:** to visible Appearance, Move therefore O you Spirit **N:**

---

[36] This is an Enochian term, being Mad-Zilodarp, meaning *"The God of Stretch Forth and Conquer"*!

[37] I.e. Sabaoth.

Come away and appear you visibly unto us, in fair & decent form in these Glass Receptacles or otherwise out of the same, in like form, visibly here before us, not in any wise terrible or affrightful unto us, to amaze or surprise us, or in any violent or turbulent manner, hurtful to us or this place, or to any other person or place whatsoever, but come & appear you in all serenity, peace & mildness, showing forth likewise unto us, a visible sign or test foregoing your appearance, and by the virtue, power, efficacy & influence of these great, mighty & sacred names of the most high God, which Adam heard & spoke, & by the Name **Agla**, *which Lot heard & was saved with his family; and by the Name of* **Gin**, *which Noah heard & spoke, after he was delivered from the Flood, And by the Names which Abraham heard & did know God, & by the Name* **Ioth**, *which Jacob heard & was delivered from the hand of his brother Esau. And by the Name* **Tetragrammaton**, *which he heard of the Angel striving with him, And by the Name* **Anapheketon**, *which Aaron heard and speaking was made wise, And by the Name* **Zebioth**, *which Moses named, & the water of Egypt was turned into blood, And by the Name* **Escherie Oriston**, *which Moses named & all the Rivers belched out Frogs, & they went into the Egyptian Houses, destroying all things, And by the Name* **Adonay**, *which Moses named, & there were Locusts appeared upon the Land of the Egyptians, & ate up all that which was remaining, And by the name* **Elion**, *which Moses named, & there was such a Storm of Hail as was not from the beginning of the World.*

And by the Name **PrimaVmaton**,[38] & the most wonderful power & efficacy thereof, which Moses named, & the Earth opened her mouth, & swallowed up Corah, Dathan & Abiram, & all their Generation & People, And by the Name that Moses heard from the midst of the burning Bush, & was astonished, And by the Name that the Israelites heard upon the Mount Sinai, & they died for fear, And by the Name **Burne**, by the virtue & power whereof the Sea parted in sunder, And by the efficacy of that Name, at the rehearsing whereof the Waters was divided, And by the mighty power of that great Name, at the speaking whereof, the Storms burst & relented.

And by the Name **Schemes**, **Amathia**, which Joshua named, & the Sun stayed his course, And by the Name **Alpha & Omega**, which Daniel named & destroyed Baal & the Dragon, And by the Name **Emanuel**, which the three Children, Shadrach, Mesack & Abednigo sang in the midst of the burning fiery furnace, & were unharmed.

And by the virtue & power of those Names, whereby Solomon called forth, constrained, bound, enclosed or shut up Spirits **Elbrach**, **Ebanher**, **Agla**, **Goth**, **Ioth**, **Othie**, **Venoch**, **Nabrach**, And by the Imperial Throne, & by the Majesty & Deity of the Almighty, Everlasting & true God of Hosts; We do call upon you, O you Spirit who is called **N:** And being dignified by the power of the holy Spirit, & strengthened by his all powerful arms, & being thereby supported with his Celestial & Divine assistance, Do Conjure, Command,

---

[38] Ashmole wrote 'Primeumaton' as 'PrimaVmaton', stressing the central 'u' so that it becomes a capital 'V'. This may have been to stress the pronunciation which was probably 'prime-you-ma-ton'. This ensures the meaning 'First Breath' or 'prime pneuma' is fully implied.

*Constrain, Call forth & move you O you Spirit **N:** to visible appearance:*

*Move therefore & appear you, & show your self visibly & affably in fair & decent form, in these Glass Receptacles or otherwise out of the same here before us, as may be most convenient & necessary, for this our purpose, in these present Operations & affairs, & come ye in all serenity, mildness, peace & friendship, & in no wise terrible or hurtful to us or to this place, or to any other place or person whatsoever, & make true & faithful answers unto all such, of these our demands & requests, as lyeth her before us, ready to be proposed, & made known unto you, & likewise readily & willingly fulfil & perform all such our other Commandments & desires, as we shall yet further wish & enjoin you, wherein your Orders & Offices, is in any wise properly appertaining & concerned, Now therefore O you Spirit **N:** prepare ye & be not obstinate, infractory or pertinacious, but come ye away forthwith & immediately from your Orders, or from what Mansion, Element, Angle, part or place of residence, or else wheresoever you are in, or at this present shall, or may, either chance by, or otherwise by divine or superior command or appointment happen to be, & depart ye not from our presence & commands, until ye have fully & effectually fulfilled our desires, in all fidelity reality & truth, without any delay, fraud, guile, or illusion whatsoever.*

*Now therefore hearken unto our cry: O ye Spirit **N:** & be not obstinate, infractory or disobedient. Know ye that we the servants of the most high God, being dignified, fortified & supported assisted & encouraged, by his omnipotent, divine, & Celestial power, & by the virtue force influence & efficacy thereof; & by this his most high, great, & mighty Name **Jehovah Tetragrammaton**, who saith & it is done; whom all*

Creatures both Celestial, Elemental & Infernal, with fear & reverence doth most humbly serve honour & obey, & wherein all the world was formed, which being heard the Elements Thunder, the Air is Shaken, the Sea goes back, the Fire is quenched, the Earth trembleth, & all the heavenly, earthly & infernal Hosts do tremble & are troubled;

*Do Conjure, Command, Compel, Constrain, Call forth, & move you to visible appearance, wherefore O ye Spirit **N:** now presently & without any further tarrying, illusion, hindrance, or delay, move ye immediately, even at this very instant Call, make haste, & wheresoever you are, come away & appear ye visibly, affably courteously & peaceably, in fair & decent form, in these Glass Receptacles or otherwise out of them, as may be most convenient & befitting this our present action, occasion, operation & affair, plainly here before us, & to show forth unto us a true & visible sign, foregoing your coming & appearance:*

And come ye in all serenity, quietness and friendship, without noise or turbulence, or in any violent manner, hurtful to us or this place, or to any other place or person whatsoever, or otherwise, either to assault surprise or amaze us, either in Spirit or bodily senses, with fear astonishment or otherwise dreadful or terrible visions, or false motions or appearances, in any wise to affright, obstruct or delude us, & make us rational, true & faithful answers, speaking so plainly unto us, as that we may perfectly hear & understand you, readily & willingly fulfilling all our demands & requests, & accomplishing all such our desires, & assisting us in these & all others our operations & affairs, in any wise relating to your nature, degree, Order & Office, & therein to perform unto us, not only what we have to propose, but also in whatsoever wise we shall further enjoin or command you.

Move therefore & come away, in the name of the Omnipotent, Everliving & true God **Helioren**,[39] & appear you as aforesaid visibly here before us, in these Names **Aye Saraye, Aye Saraye, Aye Saraye**, make haste & defer not your coming, in & through these Names **Eloye, Archima Rabur** and obey your Master who is called **Octinomos**.[40] Now then finally know you, O you Spirit **N:** that we being dignified by Celestial power, do by the Content of this our great & royal Invocation (as aforesaid) & by the virtue, power, Influence & efficacy thereof, Conjure, Command, Compel, Constrain, Call forth & move you to visible appearance, immediately at this very minute.

Give ye now therefore present audience attendance and obedience thereunto, & come away with speed, & appear ye visibly unto the sight of our Eyes, in fair & decent forms, in these Glass Receptacles or otherwise thereout here before us, & show forth unto us a visible sign foregoing your Appearance, persisting herein, to the full and effectual accomplishment & fulfilling of all our demands & requests, that we have or shall make unto you, even to the very utmost (as we have before said) without further Apology, excuse, pretence, hindrance, tarrying, delay, delusion, deceit, subtlety, Craft, disguise, interruption, false motion, disturbance, fear, fright, amazement: by any dreadful or terrible assault or surprisal, or any other Illusion whatsoever, &c.

---

[39] This divine name is found in the *Heptameron*, which is clearly the source of this part of the invocation, as it is the source of the phrase *"by the virtue of these names; Aye Saraye, Aye Saraye; defer not to come, by the eternal names of the living and true God, Eloy, Archima, Rabur"*, which is nearly identical to the wording herein.

[40] This name is found in the *Heptameron*, as part of the same presentation of the pentacle to the spirits mentioned in the previous note.

An Experiment to Cause a Thief to Return

An excellent & approved Experiment, to cause a Thief to come again with the Goods he hath stolen; & to cause any Fugitive to return again. Proved.

There are 4 Kings which reign in the 4 parts of the World, that is East, West, North & South; under which 4 Kings are 4 Spirits (as it were Bishops) the power of the said 4 Kings, are in the 4 Elements, that is, Fire, Air, Earth & Water; & these Spirits have power to bring back a Thief, Fugitive or Runaway, which soever the Exorcist pleaseth, at the reading of the Exposition:

The names of the 4 Kings	Urinuo, or Oriens, Plyomn or Paymon, Egyn, Amaymon,	King of the	East, West, North, South.
The Names of the 4 Bishops	Theltryon, Sperion, Mayerion, Boytheon,	In the	East, West, North, South.

Here beginneth the Method of this Experiment as follows:

Observe when the Moon is in the Increase, not Contrast, & the Air serene & Still, on a Monday or

Wednesday; at the Sun rising enter the sacred place, & approach the Altar, & there humbly upon thy Knees Ejaculate[41] to God Almighty, humbly confessing thy manifold Transgressions, craving Pardon & Absolution for the same. And let this be thy Care, at the least once or twice a week, on Mondays and Wednesdays as aforesaid, according to your Situation, At the end whereof you shall say the Prayer following, & after that as followeth in Order. Then put off your Habit or Vestment, & put out your Tapers, & then make a Plate of Lead in manner & form as followeth,[42] & write the Name of the four Spirits with their Characters in the extremity of each Square thereof (viz) **Theltryon** on the East,[43] **Sperion** on the West, **Mayerion** on the North, **Boytheon** on the South, and then round about under them the name of the Goods stolen, & the owners name thereof, or the Fugitive or Runaway's name; & in the midst of the said Plate write the Name **Sheho**: then make 4 little Plates, & write thereon severally, the name of each Spirit as aforesaid by himself, with his Character; & when you have rightly prepared & fitted these things ready, go to a Wood or some private place unfrequented, & make (or have in readiness) the following Circle: & then at a little distance, with bended knees & good devotion, say the Prayer following, being the same before mentioned, to be said at the Altar after you made Confession and Ejaculation, the Ruler followeth after the Plate & Circle.

---

[41] This obviously refers to a sense of hurling the words out of your mouth, not any other connotation.

[42] This use of a lead plate parallels the defixiones or binding curses which were popular in ancient Greece.

[43] The Demon Bishops seem to be unique to this MSS.

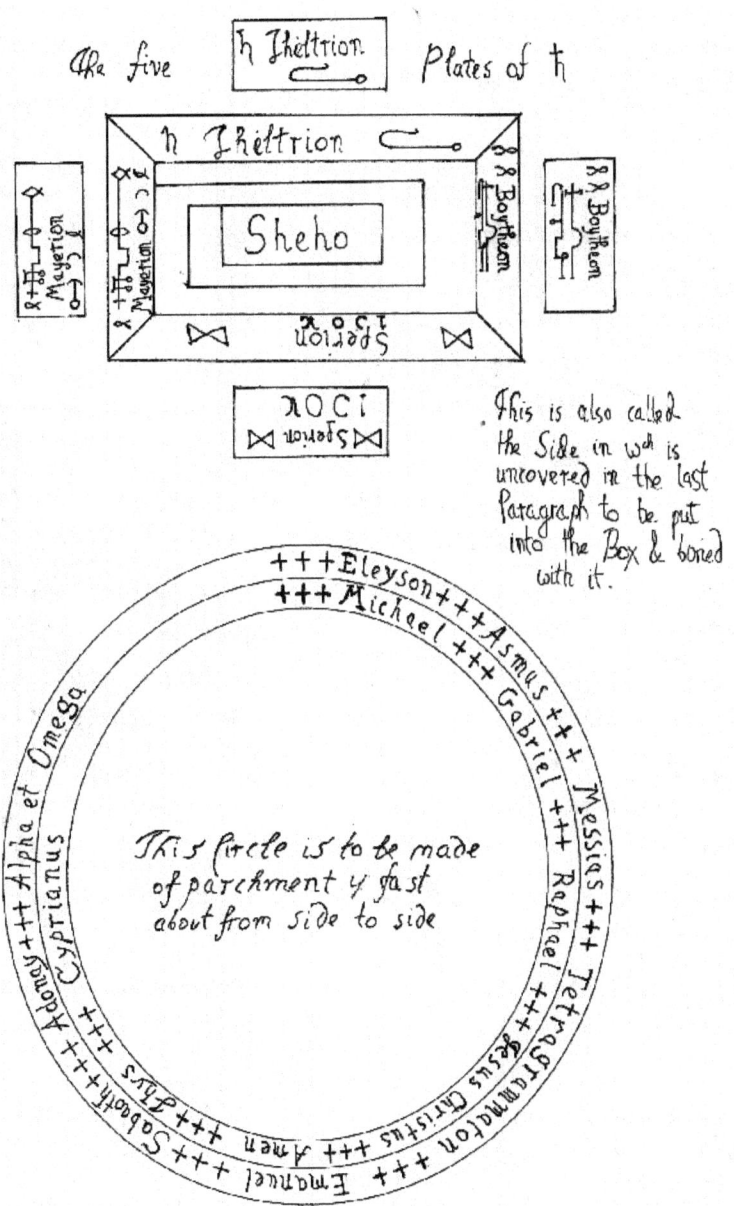

THE FIVE LEAD PLATES & MAGIC CIRCLE

The Prayer

O Almighty **Jehovah**, O **Tetragrammaton**, O **Messiah**, O **Sother, Emanuel, Alpha & Omega**, Father Son & holy Ghost, three persons & one God in Trinity & Unity, We do beseech thee for the Love thou bearest to Mankind; hear us & grant us our requests for the Marvels of thy mercies sake hear us, for thy Bitter passions sake hear us, for thy body & Blood sake hear us, for all the Charitable desires that ever thou hadst to Mankind hear us & grant us our request.

First forgive us our sins good Lord, whatsoever we have committed by though word or deed, since we came into this miserable world, unto this present hour, & ever hereafter. Grant O Lord that I may have from thee the power of thy holy Spirit, to Call, to Compel, to Constrain & Command, all Spirits both Aerial, Terrestrial & Infernal, that they with all readiness & submission yield due obedience to my Conjuration, And that they may be by me compelled to fulfil my will & desires, whatsoever I shall command them, according to thy heavenly will & gracious permission at all times & in all places, & in all days & hours, & that I may force them with all meekness & humility & expiation, readily & willingly to perform & fulfil whatsoever I shall command them to do, without fraud or delay, & more especially these 4 Spirits **Theltrion, Sperion, Mayerion, & Boytheon**, & that I may constrain them to attend on any Man or woman, that hath stolen any manner of Goods or Chattels, that they may cause the same to be brought again: & any Runaway or Fugitive to return again. This grant O heavenly God, for Jesus Christ his Son, to whom *with thee & the holy ghost, be all honour praise & glory, from this time forth, & for all time. Amen*

Then rise upon thy feet & enter the Circle, & turn your face to the East, & with good confidence Courage & Resolution, say the Conjuration following.

O ye Spirits & Devils, **Sathan**, **Lucifer**, **Beelzebub** *&* **Dansiation**; *I conjure you all by your powers & strengths you are permitted to have, by Almighty God the Father, the Son & the Holy Ghost, three persons & one God, in Trinity & unity, That you enforce these 4 Kings of the 4 Gates of the World, that is* **Urinus** *or* **Oriens** *King of the East,* **Paymon** *King of the West,* **Amaymon** *King of the South, &* **Egin** *King of the North, I conjure & potently call upon you, and Command all you Spirits & Devils* **Lucifer**, **Sathan**, **Beelzebub** *&* **Dansiation**, **Urinus** *or* **Oriens**, **Paymon**, **Amaymon**, *&* **Egin**, *by the Love, power, strength & glory of the Omnipotent & ever living God, & by all that even God made in heaven in hell, Fire, Air, Earth & Water, & in all other places, And by the Angels, Archangels, Thrones, Dominations, Principalities, Potestates, Virtues, Cherubims & Seraphims, and by all the Orders of the Angels, & by all the Saints of God, & by our Lord Jesus Christ, and by all the holy & blessed Company of Heaven, which sing continually Holy Holy Holy Lord God of Sabaoth, Heaven & Earth is full of thy glorious Majesty,*

That all you may compel & constrain with all the force you have, these 4 Spirits, **Theltrion**, **Sperion**, **Mayerion**, *&* **Boytheon**, *wheresoever they be, in Fire, Water, Air, Earth or Hell, or being bound to any man, that they nor none of them, do never sit in their places, but obey my Will & commandments in every respect both nights & days, hours &*

times, And I conjure all you Spirits aforesaid: in & by all the holy great & glorious names of God, & of our Lord Jesus Christ, spoken of in all Conjurations, Adjurations & Constringations, in any Tongue, Speech or Language whatsoever, That you all & every one of you, jointly & severally, do compel, constrain & command the 4 Spirits **Theltrion, Sperion, Mayerion,** *&* **Boytheon** *to attend on my Calls, Conjurations, Adjurations & Constraingations, in & for the fulfilling & accomplishing of my will & desires, for the obtaining of all Thefts & Thieves, Fugitives & Runaways, Goods, Chattels, Money or things stolen or strayed and Runaway, or conveyed from any man woman or child, be they moveable or immoveable Goods, Silver, what or whatsoever thing it be, that is ordained by God for Man, the same may be brought again, & for bringing back again of Fugitives or Runaways, wheresoever they be gone, run, or hidden; & this I conjure, adjure, command & compel all you Spirits or devils,* **Sathan, Lucifer, Beelzebub, Dansiation, Urinus** *or* **Oriens, Paymon, Amaymon** *&* **Egin,** *by Jesus Christ the Son Of God, and by his bitter gains & passion that he suffered for the redemption of Mankind, To whom with the Father & the Son & holy Ghost, be all honour & glory for ever & ever Amen.*

After which you shall make the Conjuration following, with good Courage & Confidence.

O ye Spirits **Theltrion, Sperion, Mayerion,** *&* **Boytheon** *whose names are here written, I exorcise, Conjure, bind; command & constrain you, by the most holy, true, just, powerful, Merciful, omnipotent & everliving God, & by his great excellent efficacious & ineffable name* **Jehovah,** *wherein the Patriarchs & Prophets have called upon him & he hath* helped them & made appear the arms & power of his strength in them admirably, seen beyond all humans expectation, And in the Name & by the Glory & dignity of our Lord & Saviour Jesus Christ, who Sitteth at the right hand of the Father, making intercision for us whose Saints we are, & through whose goodness & mercy hath authority & command over all Spirits, both Aerial, Terrestrial, & Infernal.

Whereupon know all you Spirits **Theltrion** in the East, **Sperion** in the West, **Mayerion** in the North & **Boytheon** in the South, That I potently and strongly command & conjure you, in & by all the holy Names of God, & of our Lord **Jesus Christ El Ya**, **Saday**, **Elohim Escheria**, **Agla**, **On**, **Tetragrammaton**, **Sabaoth**, **Adonay**, **Elion**, **Elyezer**, **Ananisapta**, **Messias**, **Sother**, **Emanuel**, **Alpha & Omega**, and by all the other Names & Attributes, that are, or can be said of God, & of our Lord Jesus Christ, and by the most ineffable, Celestial and unspeakable virtues thereof; And by all the Prophets, Patriarchs, Disciples, Apostles, Saints, Martyrs, Innocents & Elect of God, And by the 4 Evangelists: Matthew, Mark, Luke & John, & by their virtues & powers. And by the Angels, Archangels, Thrones, Dominations, Principalities, Potestates, Virtues, Cherubim & Seraphim, & by all the Orders of them, & by their virtues & powers, & by Heaven & by Earth, by the Sun & by the Moon & Stars & by the Crystal Sea, & by all their Virtues & powers I call upon you that you give audience & attendance to this my potent & powerful Conjuration & Call, And give obedience to my Command & to the words of my mouth, & that you do fully & effectually perform & fulfil my will & desire, in all these things which I shall request & demand of you, without hurt or damage, to me or any that appertain to me, either bodily or ghostly.

*Also I conjure you by your Kings whom you are bound to obey, & by the Chains of Solomon, & by your Seals & Characters, firmly binding, & the virtues & powers thereof; And by the virtues & powers of all Celestial, Terrestrial & Infernal creatures, I do further & again Exorcise, Adjure, command, bind & constrain you Spirits, **Theltrion**, **Sperion**, **Mayerion**, & **Boytheon**, by the virtue & power of this potent, strong & efficacious Conjuration aforesaid: and by all the royal words & sentences therein contained, that wheresoever you be, either in fire or water, Air or Earth, or being bound to any one, you forthwith give your present attendance, hereunto, willingly, peaceably & without any fraud, hindrance or tarrying, & come from all parts & places both remote & adjacent, & hearken unto my charge & request, which I shall straightly & strictly charge & command all ye Spirits **Theltrion** in the East, **Sperion** in the West, **Mayerion** in the North & **Boytheon** in the South, that you go into the place where (here you are to make known your will & desire what you would have effected)*

And that you enforce them, & let them take no rest, day nor night, sleeping nor waking, standing nor going, working nor playing, at home nor abroad, nor in any place or action whatsoever, neither in riding, running, nor sitting still, but that they may be continually tormented or troubled in their will, Limbs, sinews & bones, And that you be continually crimping & creeping upon them & about them, until he do & Return every thing herein contained be by you, or some one of you, jointly & severally ratified, fulfilled, confirmed & performed, according as it is here written on this plate of Lead, the which I bury in a place, & so leave it, or my charge & demand, signifying what I would you should do for me, it being a just & true matter, & which I charge and constrain you to do forthwith at my putting this Plate of Lead into the Earth, & every one of your Names & seals or Characters, jointly & Severally here annexed, the which you are bound to obey, Wherefore depart you & fulfil all these things as I have here commanded you & written on this plate of Lead, & effectually perform them by signs & testimonies, as you will answer the contrary to him who shall come to judge the quick & the dead & the world by Fire, & so the grace of God be between you & us, in the name of the Father Son & holy Ghost Amen.

Then bury the Plate in the Earth, putting every Spirit in his place or quarter, the great Plate in the middle, & each little plate on each quarter thereof according to his respective name & place, & you shall cover them close from Sun & Wind, & the work will not fail, for within a short or convenient space after, your desire will be effected: *probatim est.*[44]

A Constraint for a Thief or Thieves, belonging to these five Plates before mentioned; that if he will not bring the Goods or Thief to the Owner, &c:

---

[44] *"It is proven"*.

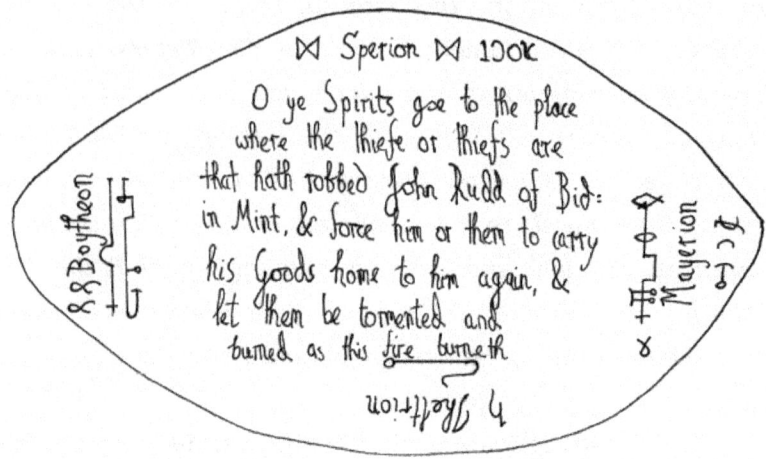

THE PLATE OF LEAD

You must make a Plate of Lead in an Oval form:[45] & fit it for a Box, & the Box must be black within & without & you must write on the Plate as you see in this figure, then draw the picture of a naked man on parchment & make it big enough to write on the Breast & Belly, Thief or Thieves; *Come to this place:*

This must be pasted on the back side of the Plate you write the names of the Goods on.

O all ye Spirits Theltrion, Sperion, Boytheon & Mayerion, & enforce the Thief or Thieves wheresoever they be, that hath robbed or stolen such things or goods from (N:) in such a place.

Then say as followeth

Almighty God, as thou knowest this is sin, & contrary to thy Laws & commandments, grant what I here shall desire.

---

[45] The name of the victim being John Rudd does further emphasise that this material is connected to Dr Thomas Rudd.

Thou Thief or Thieves, whatsoever & wheresoever thou or you be, that have stolen those things or linen, or whatsoever it be, from (N) in Such a place, at such a time; contrary to the Commandments of the Almighty God the Father of our Lord Jesus Christ, where thou be, I charge you Spirits **Theltrion, Sperion, Mayerion** *&* **Boytheon** *ruling in the 4 quarters of the world, to enforce the Thief or Thieves within an hour to return with the Goods, or confess the same, that he or they may be forgiven; if they be past having, or else until they have done so, I commit all you 4 Spirits, by the name of Jesus Christ, into the hands of those Spirits infernal of the worst sort that may be, to be tormented, And I command you & all of you & every one of you* **Lucifer, Beelzebub, Sathan** *&* **Dansiation** *to torment them, & I do by & with the force of God, charge & also Conjure you by God the Father, & God the Son, & by God the Holy Ghost, And by all that ever God made in Heaven & in the Earth, & by his Passion by his Resurrection, & by his Ascension, that ye 4 Spirits* **Theltrion** *in the East,* **Sperion** *in the West,* **Mayerion** *in the North &* **Boytheon** *in the South[46], that ye fully go to possess & torment these Thieves until they return with the Goods to (N) in such a place if they have them not to confess the same, or else again I will & commit you to* **Lucifer, Beelzebub, Sathan** *&* **Dansiation***, & by them to be buried with fire & brimstone & never to rest, waking nor sleeping, eating nor drinking, nor walking, but to be continually in most Extreme and intolerable torment, until you do presently & forthwith, cause the Thief or Thieves to return with the Goods,*

---

[46] The MSS contains a mistake here, transposing Mayerion to the South and Boytheon to the North, which is inconsistent with the rest of the text and has been rectified.

or to confess the same openly, the stolen things aforesaid & intended, and if you do not fulfil my will & desire, that you may always abide in these infernal Spirits hands, to be tormented continually vehemently & unspeakably, & that you burn both in body & mind, even as do these your names & characters in this material fire of Brimstone & other stinking things, in such a bitter & tormenting manner as is aforesaid, until you have caused the Thief or Thieves, either to return the things, or to acknowledge the Theft.

(then Cross the Fire & say)

and that in the Name[47] + of the + Father + & of the + Son + & of the + Holy Ghost + Amen + Amen + Amen +

Then say; *let God arise, & his Enemies shall be scattered.*

Then say *the Lord* & pray thus,

Lord have mercy upon us, & grant us the knowledge of these things, for our only Redeemers sake saviour Jesus + Christ + Amen + Amen + Amen +

NB that you must wait the hour you assign (or to the end of the time you assign for the return, if it be half a day) & then returning again towards the expiration thing, say over the last prayer, & towards the end thereof add these words

(*and that you burn both in body & mind as do these Names*)

then if the Goods be not brought back &c; burn the Box and show the Ashes below the Plate, & so Bury them.

---

[47] The sign + in the text indicates the magician should make the sign of the cross.

The order of placing the Plates of Lead, at the time when you bury them.

First, lay down in the earth, that Plate whereon the Names of the Goods &c are written, & let the naked man be placed next to the Earth.[48]

Note that the 4 little plates containing the names of the 4 Bishops (being cut off from the Large square Plate) must be placed upon the extremity of the 4 Sides of the written plate to face the 4 Bishops, Theltrion, &c.

Then lay the great engraved Plate upon them, the engravings downward,

Then lay the face of the Oval engraved Plate, to the back of the great engraved Plate, & so bury them.

Materials to fill the Box with

First fill the Box with Brimstone & Also fetid or other stinking matter beaten small & then take bits of Parchment, bits of Leather, & feathers & lay them towards the Top of the Box, with the Seal drawn again Velum also, and wind it about with wires to keep it close, let the wires have a lock on the top, wherein to put the point of a Sword, by which it must be held up, over a fire of Eglantine,[49] & so let it burn & consume.

---

[48] I.e. on the bottom.
[49] Eglantine Rose (*Rosa Rubiginosa*), also known as Sweet Briar.

The Consecrations & Benedictions

The Consecrations & Benedictions: And first of the Benediction of the Circle.[50]

When the Circle is rightly perfected, sprinkle the same with Holy or Purging Water, and say, *Thou shalt purge me with Hyssop, O Lord, & I shall be clean: thou shalt wash me & I shall be whiter then Snow.*

The Benediction of Perfumes.

The God of Abraham, God of Isaac, God of Jacob, bless here the creatures of these kinds, that they may fill up the power & virtue of their Odours, so that neither the Enemy nor any false Imagination, may be able to enter into them, through our Lord Jesus Christ Amen.

Then let them be sprinkled with Holy Water.

The Exorcism of Fire upon which the Perfumes are to be put.

The fire which is to be used for Fumigations, is to be in a new vessel of Copper[51] or Iron, & let it be exorcised after this manner,

I exorcise thee O thou Creature of Fire, by him by whom all things are made; That forthwith thou cast away every

---

[50] This section begins the excerpt from the *Heptameron*.
[51] T: *"Earth"*.

phantasm from thee; that it shall not be able to do any hurt in any thing; but bless O Lord this Creature of Fire & sanctify it, that it may be blessed, to set forth the praise of thy holy Name, that no hurt may come to the Exorcisers or Spectators: through our Lord Jesus Christ Amen.

Of the Garment and Pentacle.

Let it be a Priests Garment, if it can be, but if it cannot be had,[52] let it be of Linen & clean. Then take this Pentacle made in the day & hour of Mercury, (the Moon increasing) written in parchment of kidskin, but first let there be said over it, the Mass of the Holy Ghost, & let it be sprinkled with water of Baptism.[53]

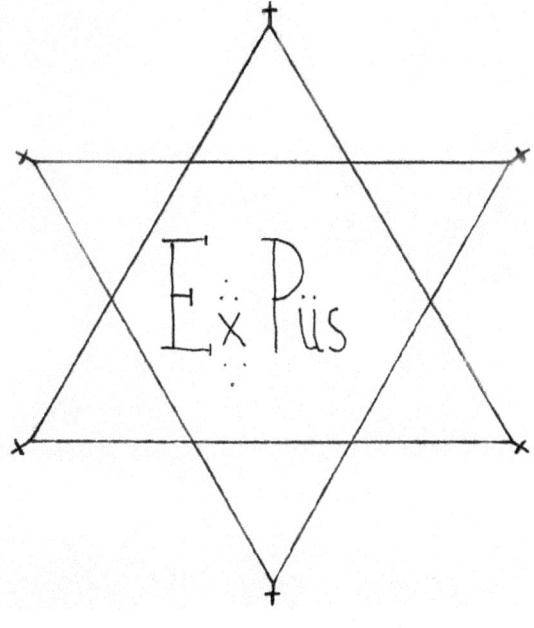

THE PENTACLE

---

[52] This phrase, *"but if it cannot be had"*, is an addition to the text.
[53] Note this is a simplified version of the one found in the *Heptameron*.

An Oration to be said, when the Vesture is put on.

Ancor Amacor Amades[54] Theodonias, Anitor, by the merits of thy Angels O Lord, I will put on the Garments of Salvation, that this which I desire I may bring to effect, through the most holy Adonay, whose kingdom endureth for ever & ever. Amen.

When you would begin to work any great Experiment[55] Let the Moon be increasing and equal & not combust. The Magical Operator or Sophy Master of the Art, ought to be clean & purified by the space of nine days before the beginning of the work. And to confess & acknowledge his mind to God,[56] and let him have ready the Perfume appropriated to the day wherein he would perform the work, He must also have Water of Baptism,[57] & a new Copper[58] vessel with fire, a Vesture & Pentacle, And let all these things be rightly & duly consecrated & prepared. Let one of the Company[59] carry the Copper[60] vessel full of fire & the perfumes, And let another bear the Book, another the Garment & Pentacle, and let the Master carry the Sword; over which there must be said an Harmony[61] of the Holy Ghost, and on the middle of the Sword let there be written this name **Agla** +, and on the other side thereof the name +

---

[54] T: *"Amides"*.
[55] T: *"Of the manner of working"*.
[56] T: *"receive the holy Communion"*.
[57] T: *"holy water from a Priest"*.
[58] T: *"earthen"*.
[59] T: *"servants"*.
[60] T: *"earthen"*.
[61] T: *"one mass"*.

On ✠. And as he goeth to the consecrated place, let him continually praise God,[62] the Company[63] answering, And when he cometh to the place where he would enter[64] the Circle with gravity and sound Judgement, Let him begin his Action being clothed with pure Garments and furnished with Pentacles, perfume and all things necessary hereunto, let him enter the Circle and call the Angels from the four parts of the World, which do govern the seven Planets, the seven days of the Week: Then call upon the angels from the four parts of the World that rule the Air, the same day wherein he doth work or experiment, having implored especially all the Names & Spirits, say as followeth

O all ye Spirits whom I have invocated, moved, and called upon, I conjure & command you all by the Name **Adon** *per* **Hagios, Otheos, Ischyros, Athanatos, Paracletos, Alpha & Omega**, *and by the sacred names* **Agla, On, Tetragrammaton**, *grant and fulfil my desires.*[65]

Thus far being performed proceed to the Conjuration and Invocation, for the day of your Action, but if they be pertinacious and infractory & will not yield themselves obedient, neither to the Conjuration assigned to the day, nor

---

[62] T: *"read Litanies"*.

[63] T: *"servants"*.

[64] T: *"will erect the Circle, let him draw the lines of the Circle, as we have before taught: and after he hath made it, let him sprinkle the Circle with holy water, saying, Asperges me Domine, &c. [Wash me O Lord, &c.] The Master therefore ought to be purified with fasting, chastity, and abstinency from all luxury the space of three whole days before the day of the operation. And on the day that he would do the work"*.

[65] This section was reproduced in Latin in Turner's edition. The conjuration is also found in the *Lemegeton*, and here we should note that this seems to be derived from the Second Conjuration. Sloane MS 3825 has the name *"Otheos"* rather than *"O Theos"*, again suggesting commonality.

to the Prayers before made, then use the Invocation following[66]

[67]*We being made after the Image of God, endued with power from God, & made after his Will, do Exorcise you by the most mighty & powerful name of God **El**, strong and wonderful, O you Spirit **Vassago** or **Usago**; we command you by him, who said the word & it was done, and by all the Names of God, & by the Name **Adonay**, **El**, **Elohim**, **Eloe**, **Zebaoth**, **Elion**, **Eserchie**, **Jah**, **Tetragrammaton**, **Sadai**, Lord God most high, we Exorcise you & powerfully command you forthwith to appear unto us here before this Circle in a fair human shape without any deformity or tortuosity; come ye all such, because we command you, by the name **Y** and **U**, which Adam heard & spoke, and by the Name of God **Agla**, which Lot heard [and was saved with his family; and by the name **Ioth**][68] which Jacob heard from the Angel wrestling with him, & was delivered from the hand of his Brother Esau, and by the name **Anaphexeton** which Aaron heard & spoke and was made wise; and by the Name **Zebaoth** which Moses named, and all the Rivers and waters in the Land of Egypt[69] were turned into Blood, and by the name **Escerchie Oriston**, which Moses named & the Rivers brought forth Frogs, and they Ascended into the houses of the Egyptians, destroying all*

---

[66] T: "These things being performed, let him read the Conjuration assigned for the day wherein he maketh the experiments, as we have before spoken; but if they shall be pertinacious and refractory, and will not yield themselves obedient, neither to the Conjuration assigned to the day, nor to the prayers before made, then use the Conjurations and Exorcisms following."

[67] Again this section is in Latin in Turner's edition, though a version of it is in English in Sloane MS 3825, as the Second Conjuration of the *Goetia*.

[68] This section has been omitted, though it occurs in Turner and is seen in the General Conjuration earlier in this MSS.

[69] This is an addition, *"and waters in the Land of Egypt"*.

*things, and by the name **Elion**, which Moses named, and there was great Hail, such as hath not been since the beginning of the World, and by the name **Adonay** which Moses named, and there came up Locusts which appeared upon the whole Land of Egypt, and devoured all which the Hail had left, and by the Name **Schemes Amathia**, which Joshua called upon, & the Sun stayed his course, and by the Name **Alpha and Omega**, which Daniel named and destroyed Baal & slew the dragon, and in the name **Emmanuel**, which the three Children Shadrach, Mesach, & Abednego sang in the midst of the fiery furnace and were delivered, and by the Name **Hagios**, & by the Seal of Adonay, & by **Theos Ischyros Athanatos**, **Paracletos**, and by these three secret names, **Agla**, **On**, **Tetragrammaton**, we do adjure & contest you,*

*And by these names, & by all the other Names of the Living and true God, & by our Lord Almighty we Exorcise and command you by him that spoke the word & it was done; to whom all Creatures are obedient, and by the dreadful Judgment of God, by the uncertain Sea of Glass, which is before the face of the divine Majesty, mighty and powerful, by the four footed Beasts before the throne, having Eyes before & behind, & by the Fire round about his Throne, & by the holy Angels of Heaven, by the mighty Wisdom of God, we do powerfully Exorcise you, that you appear here before this Circle, & fulfil our will in all things which shall seem good unto us; by the seal of **Baldachia**, and by his Name **PrimaVmaton**, which Moses named, & the Earth opened & swallowed up Corah, Dathan & Abyram, and in the power of that Name **PrimaVmaton**, commanded the whole Host of Heaven;*

We Curse you, and deprive you from all your Office, Joy & Place, & do bind you in the depth of the bottomless Pit, there to remain until the day of Judgment; & we bind you into eternal Fire, and into the Lake of Fire & Brimstone, unless you forthwith appear here before this Circle to do our Will; Therefore come ye by these Names **Adonay Zebaoth**, **Adonay Amioram** come ye, come ye, **Adonay** commandeth you, **Saday** the most mighty dreadful King of Kings, whose power no Creature is able to resist, be unto you most dreadful, unless ye obey & forthwith affably appear before this Circle, let miserable Ruin & Fire unquenchable remain with you, Therefore come ye in the Name of **Adonay, Zebaoth, Adonay Amioram**, come ye, come, why stay you, hasten **Adonay, Saday,** the King of Kings commands you, **El; Aty; Titcip; Azia; Hin; Ien; Minosel; Achadan; Vay; Vaah; Ey; Haa; Eye; Exe; a; El; El; El; a; Hy; Hau; Hau; Hau; va; va; va; va;**

If they do not come at the rehearsing of these two forgoing Conjurations (but without doubt they will say on as followeth, it being a Constraint)[70]

We conjure thee spirit **N:** by all the most glorious & efficacious Names; of the most great & incomprehensible Lord God of Hosts, that you come quickly without delay, from all parts & places of the World, to make rational answers of my demands, And that visibly & affably, speaking with a Voice, Intelligible, to our Understanding (as aforesaid) we enjoin &

---

[70] This next section is material drawn from the *Goetia*, inspired in places by the *Heptameron*. The following Constraint is drawn from the *Goetia*, and we may note the suggested combination of material from the use of the phrase *"two forgoing Conjurations"* from the *Goetia*, when in fact only the Second Conjuration is used here.

constrain you spirit **N:** by all aforesaid and by the Seven Names, by which wise Solomon bound Thee and thy Fellows in a Vessel of Brass, **Adonai Prerari Tetragrammaton, Inessenfatall, Anephexeton, Pathatumon** & **Itemon**, that you appear here before this Circle; to fulfil our Will in all things that shall seem good unto us,

And if you be disobedient & refuse to come, We will in the Power, & by the power of the Name of the Superior and Everlasting Lord God,[71] who created both you & me, & all the whole World in six days, & what is contained in it **Eye Saray**, And by the power of this name **PrimaVmaton**, which commandeth the whole Host of Heaven, Curse you & deprive you from all your Office, Joy, & Place, & bind you in the depth of the bottomless Pit, there to remain unto the day of the last Judgement, and will bind you into Eternal Fire, & into the Lake of Fire & Brimstone, unless you come forthwith & appear here before this Circle to do our Will,[72] Therefore come you, in & by these holy Names **Adonay, Zeboath, Adonay, Amioram**, come you, **Adonay** commandeth you.

If you come so far, & he yet does not appear you may be sure he is sent to some other place by his King, & cannot come; and if it be so, Invocate the King as followeth to send him; but if he does not come still, then you may be sure he is bound in Chains in Hell, & he is not in the Custody of his King, & if you have a desire to call him from thence, you must rehearse the Spirits Chain, &c.

For to Invocate the King as followeth

---

[71] S: *"supreme and Everliving god"*.
[72] S: *"in all things"*.

*O you great mighty & powerful King **Amaymon**, who bears rule by the power of the supreme God **El**, over all Spirits both Superior & Inferior of the infernal Order, in the dominion of the East, We invocate & command you, by the especial & truest Name of your God, and by God that you worship & obey, & by the Seal of your Creation, & by the most mighty and powerful name of your God **Jehovah Tetragrammaton**, who cast you out of Heaven, with all other of the infernal Spirits, & by all the most powerful & great Names of God, who created Heaven & Earth & Hell, & all things contained in them, & by their powers & virtues, & by the name **PrimaVmaton**, who commandeth the whole Host of Heaven, That you cause, enforce & compel **N:** to come unto us here before this Circle in a fair & comely form, without doing any harm unto us, or any other Creature, and to answer truly & faithfully to all our Requests, That we may accomplish our will & desires, in knowing or obtaining any matter or thing, which by Office you know if proper for him to perform or accomplish, through the power of God **El**, who created & disposeth of all things both Celestial, Aerial, Terrestrial & Infernal.*

After you have invoked the King in this manner twice or thrice over, Then Conjure the Spirit you would call forth, by the aforesaid Conjurations, rehearsing them several times together, & he will come without doubt, if not at first or second time rehearsing, but if he does not come, add the Spirits Chain to the end of the aforesaid Conjuration, & he will be forced to come, if he be bound in Chains: for the Chains will break off from him, & he will be at liberty &c.

The general Curse, called the Spirits Chain, against all Spirits that Rebel.

O thou wicked & disobedient Spirit, because thou hast rebelled & not obeyed and regarded our words, which we have rehearsed, they being all most glorious & incomprehensible names of the true God, maker and creator of you & us, & all the World, We by the power of those Names, which no Creature is able to resist, do Curse you into the depth of the Bottomless Pit, & there to remain unto the day of doom in Chains of fire & brimstone unquenchable, unless you forthwith appear here before this Circle (or in this Δ Triangle) to do our Will. Therefore come peaceably & quickly in & by these Names **Adonay Zebaoth**, **Adonay**, **Amioram**; *come, come you,* **Adonay** *comandeth,*

When you have read so far, & he does not come, Then write his Name & Seal in Virgin parchment and put it into a black Box, with Brimstone Asafoetida & such things, that have a stinking strong smell & bind the Box round with a Wire, & hang it on the Sword point, & hold it over the Fire of Charcoals, & say to the Fire (it being placed toward that Quarter the spirit is to come)

[73]*We conjure you Fire, by him that made thee & all other good Creatures in the World, that thou torment, burn & consume this spirit N: everlastingly. We condemn thee thou spirit* **N:** *into Fire everlasting, because thou art disobedient and obeyed not the command, nor kept the Precepts of the Lord thy God, neither wilt thou appear to, or obey us, nor our Invocations, having thereby called you forth, who am are the Servants of the most high & imperial Lord of Hosts* **Jehovah**,

---

[73] S: *"The Conjuration of the fire"*.

and dignified & fortified, by his Celestial power and permission, neither comest thou to answer to these our proposals here made unto you, for which your averseness & contempt, you are guilty of grand disobedience & Rebellion,

And therefore we shall Excommunicate you, & destroy thy Name & Seal, which we have here enclosed in this Box, & shall burn thee in immortal fire, & bury them in immortal Oblivion, unless thou immediately come & appear visibly, affably, friendly & courteously hear unto us, before this Circle in this Δ Triangle, in a fair and comely form, & in no wise terrible, hurtful or frightful to us, or any other creature whatsoever, upon the face of the Earth: and make rational Answers to our Requests, & perform all our desires in all things, that we shall make unto you &c.

If he cometh not yet, say as followeth:

Now O thou Spirit **N:** since thou art still pertinacious & disobedient, & will not appear unto us, to answer to such things, as we should have desired of you, or would have been satisfied in &c, We do in the Name, & by the power & dignity of the Omnipotent Immortal Lord God of Hosts **Jehovah Tetragrammaton**, the only Creator of Heaven & Earth & Hell, & all that in them is, who is the marvellous disposer of all things, both visible and invisible, We Curse you & deprive you, from all your Office, Joy & Place, & do bind you in the depth of the bottomless Pit, & there to remain, until the day of the last Judgement, We say into the Lake of Fire & Brimstone, which is prepared for all rebellious disobedient, obstinate & pertinacious Spirits, Let all the Holy Company of Heaven Curse you, the Sun, Moon & Stars, the Light, & all the Host of Heaven Curse Thee, We Curse thee, into the fire unquenchable & Torments unspeakable, & as thy Name & Seal is contained in this Box, chained & bound up, and shall be choked in

Sulphurous & stinking Substance, & burnt in this material Fire, so in the Name Iehovah, by the power & dignity of these three Names **Tetragrammaton Anaphexeton** *&* **PrimaVmaton**, *cast thee O thou disobedient spirit* **N:** *into that Lake of Fire, which is prepared for the damned and cursed Spirits, and there to remain to the day of doom, and never more to be remembered of, before the face of God, which shall come to Judge the Quick & the Dead and the World by Fire.*

Here the Exorcist must put the box into the Fire

And by and by he will come, but as soon as he is come, quench the Fire that the Box is in, & make a sweet perfume, & give him a kind entertainment, showing him the Pentacle, that is at the bottom of your Vesture, covered with Linen cloth, saying.

Behold the Conclusion if you be disobedient. Behold the Pentacle of Solomon, which we have brought here before thy presence, Behold the person of the Exorcist who is called **Octinomos**, *In the midst of the Exorcism, who is armed by God & without fear, who potently invocated you, & called you to Appearance, Therefore make rational Answers to our demands, & be obedient to us your Masters, In the Name of the Lord* **Bathat** *rushing upon* **Abrac Abeor** *coming upon* **Abarer**.

Then they or he will be Obedient, & bid you ask what you will, for they are subjected by God to fulfil our desires & demands, And when they or he have appeared & showed himself humble & meek, then you are to say as followeth.

Welcome O you Spirit or Spirits, or most Noble King or Kings, we say you are welcome unto us, because we called you, through him who created both Heaven Earth & Hell, & all that is contained in them, & you have obeyed also by the same power that we called you forth, We bind you that you remain affably & visibly here before this Circle (or before this Circle) in this Δ Triangle, for constant & so long as we have occasion for you, & not to depart without our Licence, until you have faithfully & truly performed our Will, without any falsity, &c.

The Licence to depart

*O thou Spirit **N:** because thou hast very diligently answered our demands, & was very willing to come at our first Call, We do here Licence thee to depart unto thy proper place, without doing any harm, injury or danger to Man or Beast (depart I say) & be ever ready to come at our Call, being Exorcised and Conjured, by the sacred rites of Magick, We charge thee to depart peaceably & quietly, And the Peace of God be ever continued between us & thee. Amen.*

After thou hast given the Spirit Licence to depart you are not to go out of the Circle, till they be gone, and you have made Prayers to God, for the great Blessing he hath bestowed upon in granting you your desires & delivering you from the malice of the Enemy the Devil.[74]

Therefore thou shalt pray thus.
O Lord God of heaven & Earth, Creator & Maker of all things effable & ineffable, We thy most humble servants do return thee humble & hearty thanks, for thy fatherly goodness & mercies, in granting these our desires, which through thy permission, we have now obtained & received, Bind O Lord,

---

[74] This ends the material from the *Goetia* and *Heptameron*.

those things, which thou hast taught us to obtain, in our Understandings, that we may bring them forth as out of thy inexhaustible Treasury to all necessary aid, & give us grace, that we may use such thy gift & mercies humbly with fear & trembling, to thine honour & praise, & to our own comfort here on Earth, through our Lord Jesus Christ.

Gloria Patri, et Filio, et Spiritus Sancto: Sicut erat in principio et nunc et simper, et in saculo Saculorum Amen.

[EDITORIAL NOTE: The following short section is part of the original MS, and has been included as it refers to other material in Sloane MS 3825, demonstrating its original provenance as part of the same corpus of material. It refers to material not included in this book. Its significance lies in its circumstantial contribution to the question of the authorship of material published elsewhere attributed to Dr Thomas Rudd (1583-1656), which has been challenged by some as the later work of the early eighteenth century copyist Peter Smart.

Thus material in Sloane MS 3825, including the *Nine Celestial Keys of Dr Rudd*, dated 1641, and reproduced in Harley MS 6482 (1712), is shown as being by Dr Rudd by the reference in Sloane MS 3824 to *"the Isagogical Observations &c in page 79, & are noted by pages & capital Letters, where they were inserted by Dr:R:"*. Sloane MS 3824 may be dated to the period 1641-59, with specific reference made to the date 1649.

The reference to John Rudd, the victim of the theft being redressed by the demon bishops with the lead plate conjuration earlier in the manuscript, cannot be a coincidence, with the same familial surname. We know that a J Rudd wrote a letter to Sam Ward on November 10th 1609, and this may be the same person. Several years earlier on 19th October 1605, a young (22) Thomas Rudd had written to Dr John Dee on the subject of alchemical vitriol, initiating the contact between these two great magicians.]

What follows was transcribed from another MS Copy of part of this Book, which reached only to the Isagogical Observations &c in page 79, & are noted by pages & capital Letters, where they were inserted by Dr:R:[75]

Whence note that to the Title (viz: Janua Magica Reserata) there was added in the said MS a copy per Clavem Philomusis[76]

Note that I find much of this discourse copied out from the French translation of Cornelius Agrippa his Occult Philosophy, which I have noted in the Margin.[77]

---

[75] I.e. Dr Rudd. For more details of Dr Rudd see *Practical Angel Magic of Dr John Dee's Enochian Tables* (2004), *Keys to the Gateway of Magic* (2005) and *The Goetia of Dr Rudd* (2007), all Skinner and Rankine, Golden Hoard Press.

[76] *"The Key of the Lover of Wisdom"*, possibly a reference to the *Lemegeton Clavicula Salomonis Rex* (in a noticeably different handwriting) which was added to *Janua Magica Reserata* in Sloane MS 3825.

[77] This note by Ashmole refers to the subsequent material which I have omitted. Note the reference to the French translation of Agrippa, available before the English edition. The material in fo.29-90b is omitted, and continues at fo.91.

Experiment to call Spirits that Guard Treasure

An Experiment to call out Spirits, that are Keepers of treasures Trove, Either by any Artificial Enchantment magically, or otherwise by Divine Justice; & those Spirits following have power to Command them away, & cast them out; and to do whatsoever the magick philosopher Shall Command them:

Names of the Spirits
Sulphur, **Chalcos**, **Anaboth**, **Sonenel**, **Barbaros**, **Gorson**, (or **Gorzan**) **Everges**, **Mureril**, **Vassago**, **Dantelion**, **Barbasan**, **Sathan**,

The first thing the Magical Philosopher is to oberve herein, is to be well informed, or well to inform himself by all the best ways & means he Can, whether any Treasures are hidden in Such or Such a place or no, and by whom, and for what Reasons it should be hid and absconded from posterity, and whether it be kept by any Spirit commanded and Constrained thereon, by any Magical enchantment, or otherwise by Divine justice & whether by any Aerial Terrestrial Spirit:

For this is a maxim in Philosophy, That there is a great antipathy between us & Evil Spirits, & the Celestial Angels who are our governors, Protectors, & guardians, & are Continually Employed about us, according to their orders & ministries appointed them of God, Although the Evil Spirits

Striveth & Endeavoureth to imitate the Good Angels, & in all things Every way to Counterfeit them, whereby many are Deceived, whose wickedness & malice Suits with the nature of Evil spirits, of which the Good Angels being grieved forsakes them, & leaves them to their own erroneous Will & many times for the wickedness of Some person or family, the Good Angels Curses Such a person, family or House, then the Evil Spirits have power given them, to execute the justice & Decree of the most high God, whom Such Family or person hath so heinously offended then Doth the Aerial Spirit haunt, infest & trouble Such houses or places, & molest the inhabitants, terrifying and afrightening them both & other people adjacent thereto, with horrible & unusual noises, and many fearful & hideous apparitions, neither Shall Such house or inhabitant be as Quiet nor shall any of the Generation of any Such family prosper, until providence be appeased, the Curse Expiated, and the Angry Angel or Aerial Spirit Discharged, or the enchantment taken off from the Treasure, if any be there hid, & the spirit Keeping it be Discharged therefrom, & Cast out, Sent away to his place of Residence, otherwise appointed & Decreed for him & thus Doth God punish in his justice, the heinous Sins of great offenders even to the third & fourth generation.

Next you are to Consider, whether the place be haunted, or the Treasures therein Kept (if any be hidden) either by Aerial or terrestrial Spirits, or whether any Enchantment or magical Spell, or any powerful Charms; or whether otherwise Distributed by permission of Divine justice, for many heinous unpardoned Crimes of Some one person &c: all which ought to be Diligently Considered & rightly understood. The Knowledge whereof is elsewhere before Explained &c: If there be Treasures there hidden, and

Kept by an Aerial Spirit or Spirits, then these Spirits here before named are to be called upon. & made use of herein, the praxis whereof is thus:

The House or place haunted, must be Cleared of people, and should be made private; and the house or place be made void of Any Company, Except Such as are Concerned in that business, Which Brotherhood or Society so concerned, in the management of these Affairs; As the Recovery of treasure Trove, that cannot be Otherways Recovered but by this art, Must be very tacit, Silent, and private in the carrying on of their Designs, neither Squabbling or Disagreeing amongst themselves, but wholly to rest & Rely on the prudence And genuine capacity, of the Philosophic master in this Art, by whose constancy in his perseverances, assisted by the Support, Levity, taciturnity, and fidelity of a civil benevolent And Loving fraternity, his Authority is much strengthened in his Invocations, whereby all Spirits both Aerial and terrestrial (yea & Infernal also) are brought to Subjection, & willingly Serve the master, obediently doing all his will & Command, And by this means Are matters brought to a propitious Period, and Expectations, on all hands answered with a prosperous & successful issue.

The place which is thus haunted, being prepared and Set apart for Action, the master Surely knowing that there is treasures there hidden, and that it is there Kept, & also the House Haunted by Aerial Spirits, at a Convenient time or times, when all things Are Silent and Still, go to the place, & as you Enter the place, going meekly & Deliberately therein, Say as followeth:

Emanuel and in the name of God Amen

O Lord arise, help us, strengthen, dignify, be present with us, and assist us in these our Present undertakings, Illuminate us with the Light of thy Countenance, and Deliver us from all Evil, for thy most holy & Glorious name's sake, for we have heard, And we absolutely Believe, of what our forefathers hath Declared unto us, the noble works thou didst in those days, & in the old times before them. We are thy people O Lord & the sheep of thy pasture, Therefore graciously hear us, And Grant us our Requests, and let thy mercy be Showed upon us As we do put our faith In thee, Lord we believe, help our unbelief:

Then Let the master & his fellow or fellows Enter the Circle; and Invocate as followeth:

O all ye Spirits who have power given you to Execute the Commands of the Highest, both as to his justice and mercy; O all you spirits of great power, in the Keeping of Hidden treasures, and Also of Detecting, Discovering & Yielding of the Same to the Sons of men, for whose use it was principally & Primarily Decreed and Ordained; I do Exorcise and call upon all you spirits, jointly And Severally by name, **Sulphur, Chalcos, Anaboth, Sonenel, Barbaros, Gorson,** (or **Gorzan**) **Everges, Mureril, Vassago, Dantelion, Barbasan, Sathan,** *In the most high, mighty, great, glorious, efficacious and affable name of the Creator of heaven & Earth, And all what soever is therein contained both spiritual, Animal, Vegetable & mineral, And by these his secret, powerful and commanding names,* **Jah, Elohim, Agla, El, On, Tetragrammaton,** *And in name of Jesus Christ our Saviour, the only Son of God The Father Almighty, the Same Person in Sacred Trinity,* **Messiah, Sother, Emanuel, Sabaoth, Adonay, Via, Vita, Homo Primogenitus, Agnus Dei, Alphanatos, Paracletus, Alpha**

& Omega, and by all the power that The Great God of Heaven, & his Son Jesus Christ, the true Messiah hath given both to Angels And Men,

By all aforesaid I do again Exorcise, call upon, command you and Constrain you Spirits **Sulphur, Chalcos, Anaboth, Sonenel, Barbaros, Gorson,** (or **Gorzan**) **Everges, Mureril, Vassago, Dantelion, Barbasan, Sathan**; And all others, having power that you cast out all Evil Spirits, that reside within, and by Divine permission haunteth, troubleth or molesteth this place; and all or any other spirit or spirits whatsoever, that Keepeth any treasures that is hid or buried In this place, or hereabouts adjacent, and detaineth the Same from the use of the Sons of men, Servants of the highest, & Especially one, who is the first and greatest, who is called **Camret**, Duke of Strength, with all others whatsoever they be, that have power and permission to keep the treasures that are hid or Buried In this place or hereabouts near adjacent, that neither them nor any others, from this time forth hence forward, shall Keep any treasures that is hidden or buried In this place; Or Wheresoever Else it be hereabouts adjacent, but that Such spirit or spirits, of what nature order or Hierarchy Soever they are of, either Aerial, Terrestrial or Infernal, or whatsoever otherwise or howsoever it shall be Kept, Detained or Secured from the use of man, by any spirit or spirits whatsoever As is aforesaid, let them be Cast out, Dismissed and Discharged therefrom, and command and Enforce Such Spirit or Spirits as aforesaid, Keepers of any treasures that are hidden, buried, or by any ways Or means Concealed and Detained from man, to whom the proper use, right and behoof, absolutely, and by the Original & primary Decree of our God, from the beginning of Days, undeniably Belongeth and appertaineth;

*And also Enforce and constrain Such spirit or spirits as aforesaid, Readily, peaceably & gently Submit & leave Such Treasures, as are here or hereabouts adjacent, hidden, or Buried as aforesaid, bare & Nakedly Visible to us, So that we may bear the Same away for our Necessary Uses; Or Otherwise I Exorcise, earnestly urge, require & command you Spirits **Sulphur**, **Chalcos**, **Anaboth**, **Sonenel**, **Barbaros**, **Gorson**, (or **Gorzan**) **Everges**, **Mureril**, **Vassago**, **Dantelion**, **Barbasan**, **Sathan**, By & in the name of the Father, & of the Son, and of the holy spirit, that Some one or more of you as occasion shall require, Do appear Visibly unto us, either **Barbaros**, **Gorson**, **Everges**, **Mureril**, **Vassago**, or any other, Do detect and Discover wheresoever Treasures lyeth hid, buried or otherwise concealed in this house or place, or anywhere Else hereunto adjacent unto us and rightly to inform & instruct us, how to come by & recover the Same; so that we may freely without any interruption or intermission, take and bear the Same away for the Relief of our Necessities,*

*Or otherwise, again I Exorcise, Earnestly urge, Require, & command you Spirits **Sulphur**, **Chalcos**, **Anaboth**, **Sonenel**, **Barbaros**, **Gorson**, (or **Gorzan**) **Everges**, **Mureril**, **Vassago**, **Dantelion**, **Barbasan**, **Sathan** to constrain command and Enforce Someone or more of these Spirits, **Scor**, (or **Scarus**) **Roab**, **Zaym**, **Umbra**, **Gijel**, to come and bring or cause to be brought to us, hither to this place, Such Treasures wheresoever they be, that Lyeth hid, buried or any otherwise concealed and Kept from us, in this place, or anywhere Else hereabout, adjacent, or that you constrain and Enforce, Someone, or more of the Said spirits, to appear Visibly before us peaceably, modestly and in fair & Decent forms, and no ways terrible or Violent, that we may require & command* *them to Serve us herein, and to do for us, as for the Servants of the most High and Everlasting God.*

*Finally & lastly, I do again Exorcise, call upon, command and most urgently, & Earnestly require you Spirits **Sulphur**, **Chalcos**, **Anaboth**, **Sonenel**, **Barbaros**, **Gorson**, (or **Gorzan**) **Everges**, **Mureril**, **Vassago**, **Dantelion**, **Barbasan**, **Sathan**, in the name of the Sacred & Celestial trinity, and by the Birth, passion, Resurrection & ascension of our Lord Jesus Christ, That you Cast out, discharge and Dismiss the Spirit or spirits whatsoever they be, either Aerial, Terrestrial, or infernal, that haunteth, molesteth & troubleth this house or place, or that hath the Keeping of any Treasures that are hidden buried, or by any ways or means Whatsoever concealed from the Knowledge & use of man, in this House or place, or anywhere else here Adjacent here abouts, I urgently Request you to enforce and constrain them to Depart there from, and Leave the Same Visibly and openly naked to us, So that we take & bear the same away for our necessary uses,*

*Or I earnestly require & command you, to send some one or more of these spirits, **Barbaros**, **Gorson**, **Everges**, **Mureril**, or **Vassago**, to appear Visibly unto us, and to resolve, inform and instruct us, to come by & obtain the Same, And I Do by those present and the Efficacy and power thereof, And in the name of the Supreme head and Prince of your Hierarchy, or Hierarchies, Exorcise, call upon, Require, and powerfully command, either some one or all you Spirits **Barbaros**, **Gorson**, (or **Gorzan**) **Everges**, **Mureril**, **Vassago**, to appear Visibly before us, and assist us by all the best ways and means you may or Can, to cast out Such spirit or Spirits, that haunteth, infesteth, troubleth & Disquiet this house or place, or that hath the Keeping of any Treasures, that are here or here abouts near adjoining, hidden, Buried, or by any ways or* means whatsoever concealed and Detained from us, that the same may be openly Detected & Discovered to us Visibly, So that we may peaceably and quietly, without any Noise, illusions, fraud, delays or any disturbances, intermissions or interruptions whatsoever, bear the Same away and enjoy it to our benefit, according as it is from the beginning ordained for us;

And once more earnestly urge and Require you spirits, that otherwise you enforce and Constrain these Spirits **Scor**, (or **Scarus**) **Roab**, **Zaym**, **Umbra**, **Gijel**, or some one of them to come to this place And bring hither unto us & Deliver up unto us, all such treasures as are here or hereabouts wheresoever near adjoining, that are hidden Buried or any ways concealed, And I do by these Spirits And the Efficacious power thereof, potently Exorcise, charge, constrain and command you spirits **Scor**, (or **Scarus**) **Roab**, **Zaym**, **Umbra**, **Gijel**, or Some other one of you, to appear Visibly here before us in a Decent & comely shape, and no ways terribly or turbulently, to Dismay or Delude us, Come ye in all meekness & humility, and in peace and Serenity, yielding obedience to my Commands, and requests, and the fulfilling and performing the same, wherefore prepare ye, make haste & come away, and bring along with you all Such treasures as are hid, buried or any howsoever concealed, here in this house Ground or place, or anywhere Else near here and adjoining as is aforesaid

And now I Exorcise all ye Spirits aforesaid, In the name of the Everlasting And Heavenly God The Father, the Son & the Holy Ghost, & in the names and by the power of your Hierarchies, and by the imperial authority of the princes and the Heads thereof And by their Seals & Characters firmly binding & commanding, and I do Earnestly, urgently and *powerfully require and Command you all, jointly and severally by those present, that you observe, fulfil & perform all my Desires herein Contained, and to do for me in all your respective offices, as for the Servants of the Highest, without any turbulence, noise, hindrance, fraud, prolixity,[78] or delay.*

 finis

Now although this Experiment should peradventure prove to be Long in the effecting, and bringing thereof to pass, and to be a piece of tedious & tiresome practice, almost to the Disheartening and Even casting into Despair the Master & his friends; but yet never be Discouraged nor Disheartened thereat, but proceed on therein, & persevere, with faith, patience and constancy, and Doubt not but the End will be propitious, and Crown your Expectations with a happy and prosperous issue: for these spirits are by nature obstinate and perverse, and in Such an Experiment are very slow and Remiss in their appearance, and Do unwillingly obey & Submit to the Invocations & Commands of any Magician, until they are urged & constrained thereto, by the frequent motion, constant action, & the Continual Care, Diligence and prudent Management of the Master in these Affairs; such are not usual, common, nor easy, but to be overcome absolutely by faith, Constancy, patience, prudence and perseverance; always Remembering that there is an antipathetic Continual Combat, between the Celestial Angels and the Evil Spirits, wherein the Celestial Angels Vanquish by patience: If no access or freedom is to be had to the place Haunted, or where the Treasure is Supposed to be, to act and Invocate there, then recourse must be had to the

---

[78] Long-windedness.

Experiment following and particular spirits called upon, to bring Such Treasures to Such a place, Where you are or shall appoint, & So proceed that way.

Of Spirits and Fairies

We must understand, that there are terrestrial spirits or spirits Conversant upon Earth, of Several & Different Natures, [79]Some are Evil & offensive to men, and Do wander up & down in this inferior world, enraged against all, whom St Peter compares to roving Lions, & are vulgarly Called Devils, the principal whereof was an Angel, & being formed apostate, persuaded many of the Angels to Decline with him, were therefore driven & cast forth of Heaven,[80] from the order of Good Angels for their pride, which the Devilish serpent **Ophis**, who was the Head of that Rebellious Army, who to this day are therefore called his Angels, and from the Beginning of the world, the Dispensation of things, is ordained by this means, that the Executing of God's Justice (amongst the rest) upon such matters or persons, as with whom & wherewith he is Displeased, is committed to their Charge.

And these do Confess their plan being cast forth into this vale of misery, do wander up & down upon the Earth, Keeping Treasures as aforesaid, haunting & molesting Such houses & places, and vexing any that shall seek the Recovery thereof, till they are brought to a Kind of familiarity and

---

[79] This following section is largely paraphrased from Book III chapter 18 of *De Occulta Philosophia* of Agrippa.

[80] A version of the tale of the Fall of the angels from heaven, with the implication that it was part of the divine plan to effectively provide God with an earthly fallen angelic presence to conduct his will.

obedience, to deliver & give up the Same, And also otherwise to vex & terrify Earthly things, invading mines, causing of gapings of the Earth, Striking together the Foundations of mountains, terrifying & vexing not only men but also other Creatures:

And some again by several Kinds of various and Several ways of Divisions only, do contrive rather to weary men then to hurt them, Some heightening themselves to the length of a Giant's body, and again shrinking themselves up to the smallness of a pigmy[81] And So Changing themselves into Diverse forms, do disturb and astonish men with vain fear, Some wandering up & Down in the Obscure Air: Some above the seas, Rivers, Lakes, Pools & Other waters, and moist Bogs and Such like Kind of places, Some others study lies & Blasphemies, as we Read of one Saying, I will go forth and be a Lying Spirit in the mouth of all the [progeny] of Ahab.[82]

Some others who are pernicious spirits, Do lay wait and overthrow Travellers in their Journeys, and rejoice in wars and the Effusion of Blood, and afflict men with Cruel Stripes of which we Read in many places of the old & new testament, where many comparisons are made of them, and Several names attributed to them. St Matthew Saith, for fear of which no man durst pass that way, the prophet Isaiah compares them to Satyrs, Screech Owls, Sirens, Storks &c: The psalmist Compares them to Asps, Basilisks, Gorgons, Dragons, The Gospel to Scorpions, Mammon, the prince of this world, the Rulers of Darkness, and in Some places the prince of wickedness, who is Sometimes called **Beelzebub**,

---

[81] Note that Earth Elementals were referred to as Pigmies in manuscripts from this period.

[82] This is from I Kings 22:23.

sometimes **Sorapis**,[83] Sometimes **Pluto**, being the Greek name thereof, under whom amongst them, **Cerberus** is said to be chief and is called the three headed Dog, because he is conversant in the three Elements of Air, Earth, & water. And these sorts of spirits are Said to be Evil and pernicious by nature.

There are another Sort of terrestrial spirits, whose residence is upon the superficies of the Earth, who also have power to Keep hidden treasures; but then it is thus; Many times Distractions And Disturbances happen to be in a nation, and also in a family, and that the Good honest Inhabitants live in great fear, of Losing that Substance, they have Carefully got together by their great Labours or otherwise, and so to save & secure It in time of need, do usually hide or bury it in some convenient obscure place, where some or other of these spirits hath Residence, or a delight to be frequently in, & peradventure these people may not have any friend or Relations about them, that they dare with safety repose any trust or confidence in, & so they may die without making any discovery, where they have hid or Buried their Substance: the which when those Kind of spirits, who by their orders Resideth or frequently delighteth in Such a place, finding Such a thing as treasures, to be hidden, or buried there, without any owner left, immediately seize thereon. And Keep the Same &c:

Those spirits are by nature both good & bad, but Generally they are not So noxious, offensive, hurtful or vexatious, but more near to men, and are affected with human passions, Delighting much in man's Society, and do willingly Dwell with him, and will serve him well & faithfully

---

[83] Clearly a misspelling of the Greco-Egyptian God Serapis.

in all things, wherein they are entrusted, and often times do meet poor honest men, women & Children, and are willing to be very Courteous to them, to serve them, doting on such Kind of honest and harmless people, but at such unusual Sights and accidents, for want of prudence and confidence, ignorantly stand amazed and astonished, frightening themselves, being possessed with a vain fear, so then the spirit vanisheth and leaves them, which peradventure otherwise might reveal something to them, that might do them and their posterity good: Some others there be that Delight in the company of diverse domestic and wild animals, Some reside [...][84] in and about much delight to be about woods, Parks & such kind of places,[85] Some about Champion fields, some about fountains, Some about Rivers, Some about Bogs, Marshes & ponds, Some about mountains, Some about meadows, some about trees, brakes & bushes, some about flowers, some about fruit, some about Barns, Stables, Cow-houses, dovecotes, Sheepfolds, and places where Implements for Husbandry is Laid up, Some in dwelling houses, Some in one place & some in another;

All which is upon the superficies of the Earth, and places apt and convenient enough, to hide or bury money, or any other Jewels or treasury in, Safe Enough one would think, from any ones finding out, though not at all Kept by any Spirits Whatsoever; For all hidden treasures are not kept

---

[84] Unintelligible word.

[85] The following list clearly refers to the list of fairy creatures given in Sloane MS 3825, included for comparison. Fairies, Hobgoblins, Elfs (Champion fields), Naiads (Fountains), Potamides (Rivers), Nymphs (Marshes & ponds), Oreads (Mountains), Hamedes (Meadows), Dryads & Hamadryads (Woods), Satyrs & Sylvani (Trees Breaks & Bushes), Napta & Agapta (Flowers), Dodona (Acorns, fruits), Palea & Feniliae (Fodder & the Country).

by A spirit, or spirits, (Especially whilst the owners thereof are alive) though generally they are otherwise So Kept, for the reason before alleged, & those Spirits Do never Keep such noises, nor make Such hideous disturbances, nor terrify amaze & affright people with their Ghastly and strange Apparitions & Dreadful uproars, but are abundantly more mild, and the noises they make are not at all Dreadful nor Astonishing, as that of the Aerial and the other terrestrial spirits forementioned, but more softly mutely & Silently, Sometimes by Knocking at or against some Door, Wall, or table, or partition, sometimes by the Clattering of pewter, Brass, Iron, or Chairs & Stools, or working tools together, & then soon cease & Depart, it may be they may appear to some, whom they had a good liking for, willing to disclose somewhat to them, but through a vain fear Ignorantly, that benefit is Lost; At which the spirit being somewhat moved to a Kind of passion, seldom or never proffers the like again, & So may keep the Treasures hidden in such A place, firm out of mind; because it is not either Regarded, or not Rightly and Artificially Sought after;

 Some of those spirits there are, that Do Inhabit, Dwell in & Delight in Mines, & also under those mountains, and other such like places, where there is gold & silver &c: and in places where Treasures & other things are hidden: & that lie nearer to the bowels of the Earth; And these kind of spirits are said to be possessed with all temporal things And the Riches & treasures of the Earth, and are much Delighted therewith, And carefully Keep the same, and do not willingly neither part nor depart the same therefrom: Those who work & dig in mines, & Search in the Bowels of the Earth, for Such of nature's Benignities as It affordeth, have great Knowledge of these spirits; sometimes they are very

Courteous & Benevolent, & will go to the Master of mines of such works, & will Desire to work for them amongst the Rest of their Labourers, and for the same wages, and are often times by them accordingly Employed & Set on works, and prove very faithful And Laborious there, in doing such work as two men, but they will neither talk nor associate themselves with any, but when their work is Done, and their wages paid them, according to the Custom of the Master and the Labourers, away they go, & are seen no more, till they Come to work again:

& they are not to be taken notice of, nor talked to, or in the Least affronted by any workman, & those spirits being Known by very many miners, both masters & others, they do much observe them, and give Orders to all Such Other workmen, that either has no Knowledge of them, and otherwise through Ignorance apt to Displease them, to Do So to at their Perils: As other times they will forewarn the Labouring Miners, of any Dangers or Perilous accidents, that may be near and ready to befall them, as when they are heard once, twice, thrice Or oftener, to Knock[86] or strike in the same place, which foretelleth the Death of him that Dig & Labour there, if they haste not the sooner away from thence, for either they are buried by the fall of a mountain, or perish by the Suffocation of an Earth, Damp, Or some other Dangerous Accident: And at some times they are as Vexatious and Troublesome to the Laborious Diggers, molesting & persecuting them with pinches, blows and stripes, and other torments, to such which in any otherwise abuse them all: for the nature of these Kind of Terrestrial

---

[86] This is the old belief found in many mining areas of *"Knockers"*, the spirits who reside in mines.

spirits, is Really to affect & Love all those that Love them, and that Keep their words & promises, & that are just & honest in their Dealings and actions, and they hate all Such as hate & abuse them, Smiling & proclaiming and believing them to be, what in truth by nature they are not, as infernal Devils &c: these spirits never show themselves to any shape and effect, & in Love with, In any shape but what is human, and altogether indiscernible from us Mortals, but to such as they have any Antipathy to, they appear either in Several forms, which often times doth much astonish, amuse, and affright them, yet nothing So hideous or terrible As the Aerial, and the other Degree of terrestrial Spirits forespoken of, &c:

Or else they seldom or never appear to them at all &c: they are Knowing in all arts And, or Can be found out, in all the Light of nature, and contain the Knowledge of All things, and understandeth what appertaineth to the Earth, or the Studies of all In the Liberal Sciences, and in all other their Curious Arts, mysteries & Vocations, and have the Keeping and command of many Mines Royal, & of great store of treasures, hidden & buried in the Earth, and are many times beneficent to men as aforesaid, they Know the thoughts & inclinations of men in a great moment whereby It comes to pass, that we may possibly move them to come to us With far more ease and serenity, than any of the Aerial, forespoken.

Conjuration of Treasure Spirits

He who would call upon, and speak with any spirit or spirits of this order, concerning treasures Trove, or any other mineral Treasures Enclosed in the Bowels of the Earth, or the Keepers thereof (if any be) may Do It at such place or places, where they are Conversant & most frequent in, for it is most proper & significant So to do, Else a particular private place therefore be selected & made Choice of, where those spirits are either Seen or said to haunt or be frequent in, or where Treasures are supposed to be hidden, or as near it as possibly may be, and at a Convenient time, in the Evening when the night is serene, Go there & solemnly Invocate &c:

At the Entering the Circle, Say thus: *In nomine Die Altisini Creatoris omnium Rerum in Coelo, & Terra, Glory be to God on high, on Earth Peace, Good will, towards all*

Then Invocate as followeth. *O ye Spirit or Spirits, by whatsoever name, you are Called that haunteth inhabiteth this place, and frequenteth this house; Ground, or place, or that hath the Keeping of treasures hidden, Buried or otherwise concealed from and denied the Discovery and use of by the Sons of men, I do in the name of the Father & of the Son & of the holy Ghost, Exorcise, command, Constrain and most Earnestly Urge and require you, to appear visibly unto me, and my Brethren, in fair & Decent form, to show forth unto us, what we shall desire of you,*

& I do by these powers, and in the Great And most powerful names of the Immense and Almighty Creator of heaven & Earth, And all that is therein Contained, both spiritual, animal, Vegetable and mineral, Even the Incomprehensible & Ever living God, **Sabaoth**, **Adonai**, **Dominus**, **Deus**, **Erarmus**, **Otheos**, **Iskyos**, **Athanatos**, **Paracletus**, **Elohim**, **Agla**, **El**, **On**, **Tetragrammaton**, and by & in the names of his Only Begotten Son Jesus Christ, the high King & Lord of all the world, Who shall come to Judge both you & us, at the dissolution of this Earthly Fabric, **Jesus Christus**, **Messias**, **Sother**, **Emanuel**, **Alpha & Omega**, and by his Birth, Passion, Most Glorious Resurrection, & Ascension, And by the Coming of the holy Ghost, the most Sacred Comforter, I do hereby powerfully and Earnestly command, urge, and constrain you, & in the name of the Prince, & by his Seal & Characters binding most Solidly, & by the Head of your Hierarchy, and the power thereof, I most urgently Require you, to appear visibly and formally unto me, before this Circle, to inform us Concerning the Treasures that are hidden, Buried, or by what way or means soever it is otherwise Kept, & Concealed from us,

    I do therefore call upon, command, constrain and require you Spirit or spirits, of whatsoever Order you are of, or by whatsoever name as you are Called or Known by, though not Known to us, that hath the Keeping of Treasures hidden or Buried in this house, Ground or Place, or near adjacent here abouts, to appear Visibly to us, and to detect & disclose the Said hidden Treasure to us, and Either to Direct and instruct us, how to recover & take the Same away, for the Supply of our Necessities, or otherwise that you avoid and depart from the said Treasures, that are here or hereabouts adjacent, hidden, buried or otherwise concealed, and that you permit the Same & Quietly, peaceably, meekly, gently and benevolently, in all friendship and love, to Quit the Same, and to Lay it openly bare & naked to us, Visibly to the Sight of our own Eyes, and Surrender & Deliver up the Said Treasures unto us, and that you permit and suffer us to bear the same away, & to enjoy It and convert It to our Necessary uses, without hindrance or delay,

And I do, Exorcise, bind and adjure you spirit or spirits, that have the Keeping of the treasures, that are hidden or Buried in this house, Ground or place, & All other spirits whatsoever, & of whatsoever nature or order they are of, whether Aerial, Terrestrial, or Infernal, that shall be here or where the said Treasures are; who by their Visible or invisible Craft or Subtleties, shall in anywise Oppose: or Strive to hinder, or thwart us from obtaining & bearing away the Said Treasure, I do in the name of the only Almighty and heavenly God, the Great **Jehovah**, & in the name of Jesus Christ our Lord, Command, bind and Constrain you all spirits whatsoever, As aforesaid, that shall in anywise by your Crafts or Subtleties, Seek to Let or hinder from the Obtaining and bearing away of the Said Treasures, that is here or hereabouts hidden or buried, Quietly, peaceably & Gently to avoid and depart from this place, where the Said treasures are hidden or buried, and that ye tarry not, neither continue or Remain one hour longer there or thereabouts,

But I command bind and Constrain You spirits as aforesaid of &c: that shall be here or hereabouts, to Let or hinder us, from Obtaining & bearing away of the Said hidden treasures, we are seeking for, In the Name of him, who sayeth but the word and it is done, that you haste away from thence, and forthwith repair in peace to your order or place of Residence, preordained, Decreed and appointed for you: and *now I do by those Princes, and in the name of almighty God the Father the Son & the holy Ghost, discharge you: from tarrying any Longer here or hereabouts, I do Command, Charge, bind, and Constrain you spirit or spirits, that shall be here or hereabouts, or where the treasures are hidden, to Let or hinder us from obtaining & bearing away the Same, for our Requisite uses, as aforesaid, to depart & hasten away to your Orders or place of Residence, preordained & decreed for you, & I potently adjure, and command you to haste away, & Immediately begone, to your orders as aforesaid, and tarry not one hour Longer go in peace be with you Amen.*

And now I do once again in the name of the Eternal & our Everliving God, Exorcise, Call upon, and adjure you spirit or spirits, that haunteth & frequenteth this Ground, or house, or place, and that hath the Keeping of the treasures, that are hid, buried or otherwise Concealed here or hereabouts adjacent, to appear Visibly, & in fair & Decent form to us, to Instruct, Direct and verily to inform us, how to detect, discover, and obtain the treasures that are hidden or Buried In this place, or in any other place Elsewhere hereabouts; or that ye peaceably & quietly Demit & Depart from the Same, and leave it openly, bare and naked, visibly to the sight of our own Eyes, and Deliver the same to us in our possession freely, so that we may bear the Same away, and firmly without fraud, or later hindrance, or any other Crafty or Deceitful act, deed or thing to be Done, that we for Ever Enjoy the same, and Convert it to our necessary uses,

And further Know spirit or spirits aforesaid, that frequenteth and is conversant in this house, Ground or place, and that hath the Keeping of Treasures that are hidden or Buried herein or hereabouts, Know ye I say and understand, that though I call not upon you, neither by name, Knowledge or any Signature, more or otherwise than by the name of spirit or spirits, as being at present altogether unknown to us, that I call upon you with the Tongue, Heart & Spirit of faith and Confidence, for we do eagerly & sincerely believe of you, and that you are, that which our forefathers have reported and Declared to us, of you, & in all things concerning you, And of all those noble services you have done for them, and of your worthy friendship And familiarity with them, & we also absolutely believe you to be as courteous, friendly & Benevolent, to whom you please, and have love to, and that Sympathies in faith Love and Friendship with you, as you are justly Displeased and adversely obstinate to such, who are Wilful, perverse and blind Ignorance, doth not only misbelieve, and are wholly incredible of you, but also much abuse you, in their most Gross & scurrilous Language, frequent Discourses, & most abominable mistakes; all which wilful obvious scurrility, abusiveness And incredulity, we do here in the presence of heaven And Earth, and of all the Good Angels and Spirits, utterly detest and abhor, and do Absolutely protest against It as most ridiculous, impertinent & heretical &c:

Therefore we verily, absolutely & clearly believe of you, & desire friendship with you, and the help, Council & instructions, and all Such personal and visible Assistances, as we shall Rationally Require of you, according to your orders and offices appointed you of Almighty God, be pleased readily to assist us in all Such of our Terrestrial Affairs, & more Especially Concerning all hidden treasures, and mines of Gold or Silver &c: that we shall at any time ask or seek for, accordingly to your Customs and, usual formalities or as shall please and be seen your Goodness & benevolence herein, any manner of wise and in all friendship and humanity, to accommodate, instruct, assist and Serve us,

And now having thus far Declared, and in all fidelity and honest integrity without fear (as I humbly conceive) uncontrolled and unmasked our Selves, in our more Reasonable beliefs & confidence; both of you & in our affairs, & of your favourable Resolves and friendly Assistance therein, I do in the name, and by the power of the prince and head of your Hierarchies, and primarily by his, their, and your seals and Characters binding Most Solidly, Adjure, command and most Earnestly and confidently urge, request and importune you again, to move, & visibly show your Self or Selves unto us, and to Declare truly unto us, and instruct us, how we shall Discover and Recover the treasures that are hidden or Buried in this house or place, or wheresoever else it is hereabouts &c: or otherwise to bring it to this place to us, and here leave it openly bare & nakedly visible to us, & Deliver the Same Really without fraud, Deceit or any Crafty or Subtle Devices, tricks, Or other Delusions, whereby we may be as soon deprived again thereof, to us so freely And friendly, that we may certainly bear it away, for any proper uses & behoofs; And herein we Earnestly & urgently entreat you, to do for us, as for the Servants of the highest.

Let the master continue Invocating and calling upon those spirits, Every night, from Eleven of the Clock or somewhat past, until toward two; observing to give over at the break of Day, especially to follow it very Close all the Increase of the Moon, and not at all to Despair in the tediousness or prolixity thereof; And when any appearance or sign of any Appearance shall present itself, either to the master, or his Associate or Associates that are with him, And it should be moveable, and seem to float and shift itself to & fro, let the master continue his invocation until it seem to be more static, & stand before you; & by some proof, or Kind of

Signature, showeth an offer of love & friendship, and a Kind of willingness to satisfy your desires, and then shall you bind him with the Bond of spirits, if you so desire; but if any offer, seem with a voluntary success to be perceived &c: then it may be needless:

Then ask him his name, and bid him show his Seal or Character, to which he giveth obedience, & ask him to whence he belongeth, the which when he hath Declared, then propose your requests, showing them fairly written with you; when all is Done according to your desire, then Licence him to Depart &c: or &c:

We need not instance further to enlighten the understanding, or for any further, better or more Instructions to any Philosopher in this Art, touching this Subject, for if his more rational and Intelligible faculty be not genuine Enough to comprehend and improve, what is here hinted; all the instructions of men & Angels avail little, for it is a hard matter to make A silken purse of a swine's Ear, only thus far in a word we shall give to understand, that by how much the Greater the noises are heard, and visions Seen about the house or place, so much the Greater the Treasures may be judged to be, & nearer the Superficies of the Earth.

The Fairy Court and Treasure

NB There are also another sort of terrestrial spirits of the nature of these next forespoken of, that Dwell on the Superficies of the Earth, & in the Caves & Caverns thereof, who Likewise haunteth houses and other places, & have the Keeping of Treasures, that are hidden or Buried therein, who are somewhat more humane & courteous by nature than the former, and are more feminine And delight in the Company of women & Children, and more Especially of Such who are wholly inclined to housewifery, as maidservants &c: but they poor souls being by fear and ignorance also, many times affrighted & astonished, at the Least unusual Sight or Noise, of any of them, Do thereby Lose many Benefits Yet not withstanding to such as they bear Love & Kindness too, they are very benevolent and friendly &c: and are again as obnoxious and offensive to them as they hate, And they are avespertine Nocturnal wandering spirits, who many times will come to some, even from Sun Setting to its Rising the next morn:

These Kind of spirits are more frequently visible than any others, and are the Least of the Hierarchies, and where they Haunt or do Keep any hidden Treasures, they make no great matter of Noise or Disturbance; their Noise Seemeth much as the treadings of many people, & sometimes as if there were a preparation to some great feast, as if there were two or three Cooks at work in the Kitchen, and the jack going, the Bread Rolling to & fro in the Oven, and all such

Kind of Noises, as if many folks were all at work, which are not so hideous or terrible as other spirits Do make.

These spirits may be also called upon as the other, in such places where Either they haunt or foremost frequent in, and the place which is appointed or set apart for action must be Suffumigated with good Aromatic Odours, and a Clean Cloth spread on the Ground or a table nine foot Distant from the Circle, upon which there must be Either a Chicken or any Kind of small joint, or piece of meat handsomely Roasted, and a white mantle, a Basin or little Dish like a Coffee Dish of fair Running water, half a pint of Salt in a bottle, a bottle of Ale Containing a Quart, Some food and a pint of Cream in a Dish provided Ceremonies they are much pleased & delighted with; and doth allure them to friendly familiarity willingly & Readily fulfilling your desires &c: without much Difficulty, and some have used no Circle at all,[87] to the Calling of these spirits, but only being Clean was heard and apparelled, sit at another table or place only Covered with Clean Linen Cloth, nine foot Distant & so invocate.

Those Kind of Terrestrial spirits are vulgarly Called of all people generally Fairies or Elves, and the natures and Quality of them are well Known to many, those spirits there are too who are Set over the Hierarchy as the Supreme head thereof, whose names are **Mycob** and **Oberion**,[88] under whom again are Seven Sisters, placed as the next principal, whose names, Are, **Lilia**, **Rostilia**, **Foca**, **Folla**, **Africa**, **Julia**,

---

[87] The absence of a magic circle is unusual and not recommended.

[88] Oberion and Mycob are mentioned in Folger MS Vb 26 (1580), and also in several other MSS from the time, so this is not an isolated occurrence. All of these fairies are referred to in Sloane MS 3825, contextualising them.

Venulla,[89] under whom again are many Legions as Subjects and Subservient &c: who (as aforesaid) wander to & fro upon the Earth, and have the Keeping also of many Treasures that are hidden or Buried, especially such as are hidden in those places that they frequent, inhabit, or Delight in, and that Are innocently hidden by good honest people; Either for Security, or future preservation, who many times Die, & leave it so unrevealed, then are Such treasures Seized on and Kept by these terrestrial Elves; if ever they happen to come where it is &c: then the Magical Philosopher understanding, that any treasures are Kept by the terrestrial spirits of this order, And would obtain the same, and would have converse with them, let him observe the foregoing Directions, and at the appointed time repair to the place designated for action, and invocate as followeth,

I Exorcise, adjure, call upon, urge and Earnestly Require you terrestrial spirits, that are the supreme head of the Hierarchy, of those that Are called Fairies, and who are Called by the names of **Mycob** *and* **Oberyon**, *In the name of the Almighty, Everliving and heavenly God* **Jehova**, *and of his only Begotten & well beloved son Jesus Christ our Lord,* **Messias, Sother, Emanuel**, *the high King & Lord of all the world, I do hereby call upon and importunately Desiring Spirits* **Mycob** *and* **Oberyon**, *to command the Seven Sisters* **Lilia, Rostilia, Foca, Folla, Africa, Julia, Venulla**, *or some one of them, to appear visibly to us, or in Your friendly Benevolence, to send some one or other spirit or spirits, of*

---

[89] Folger MS 2250, entitled *"Spell to bind the seven sisters of the fairies to you for ever"* (c. 1600) refers to the seven fairy sisters who are found in Sloane MS 3824 and Sloane MS 3825, placing them several decades earlier.

your Hierarchy or orders, to accommodate instruct and assist us, in such of our Requests wherein they may:

The which I confidently & Earnestly importune of you as are our friends, & we are your friends, and all of us servants to the Highest in whose name I now Call upon you and humbly urge, and most Earnestly Desire you, to Send one of the Seven Sisters next subservient under you, to Appear visibly to us, & to assist us in the obtaining and recovering of their Treasures, that are hidden or Buried in the House or place, or Elsewhere adjacent hereabouts, or to send some one Subject Subservient of your Hierarchy, to Assist and help us herein, and also in all Such matters And things as we shall Desire their Instructions and accommodations in,

Wherein, they may Continue this invocation for seven nights from the Hour of Eleven till two, and invocate nine times an hour but withal observing that if Any Apparition or Vision should appear, in form and manner, willing to Commune with us, in the Interim, you may then cease, and desire to Know the name & seal of Such Spirit, and when you have taken a note thereof you may proceed to your Demands, which you ought to have fairly written Down, because then they are In A greater Readiness, and Chargeth not the memory to recollect It Self, for being So stumbled & hobbled in your conceptions, you may Chance to lose that opportunity and peradventure your Design too,[90] but If nothing happens in the interim, then after the first seven nights, always beginning the next night after the Change of

---

[90] The emphasis is on having carefully worked out any questions and demands beforehand, so they are properly crafted, and to avoid any memory lapse or glamour.

the moon, you shall invocate or call upon the Seven Sisters as followeth,

Sator Arepo Tenet Opera Rotas[91]

Kyrie Eloyson. Christe Eloyson. Kyrie Eloyson. Adonay Cui Pater Cui Filius Cui Spiritus Sanctus Allelujah.

I exorcise, adjure command constrain & most Earnestly urge and request you **Akerayes**, the Sisters of those terrestrial spirits, who are Called Fairies or Elves by & in the name of the incomprehensible God of heaven & Earth, & all Creatures whatsoever are there In Contained and Comprehended, **Jehovah, Elohim, Agla, El, Tetragrammaton**, & in the name of Jesus Christ, begotten of a Virgin by the Holy Ghost, and born in the flesh at Nazareth, the second person In trinity, And the Saviour of the World. Especially of all believers, & those who lay hold upon him by faith, Thereby Confidently and firmly laying hold on the promises, that whatsoever we Ask our Heavenly Father, or shall any ways act, or do in his name, nothing shall be Denied us, nor be impossible to us, in whose name & through whose authority[92] we as true believers do Call upon, constrain and very Confidently Urgently and Earnestly Importune you, in the name also, and by the power of the Head and Supreme of your orders, or Hierarchy, and to whom you are the next In Order, governing over many Legions of other your Subjects & Subservients or some one of you **Lilia, Rostilia, Foca, Folla, Africa, Julia, Venulla**, to appear visibly to us, or to send someone other of your Subjected Subservients to help and

---

[91] This is an interesting use, as these words are more commonly found in the Sator magic square.
[92] Word unclear in the original.

Assist us in the obtaining of the treasures that are hidden or Buried in this house or place, or Elsewhere adjacent hereabouts, And more Especially the spirit or spirits that hath the Keeping thereof, Leave, Be Discharged & quit therefrom, & so avoid the same, and forthwith to Donate, Yield up & Surrender the Same, into our possession, so that we may bear the same away, and convert it to our necessary uses, without fraud or any other Crafts or Subtleties, that may in any wise deprive us thereof,

I do once again Exorcise, adjure and command thee **Lilia** *& all thy Sisters & subjects By the imperial throne, and by the majesty & Deity of the Everliving God, that some or other spirit of your orders, and more Especially Such spirit or spirits, that have the Keeping of the treasures that are Hidden or Buried In this house or place, or near adjacent hereabouts Do appear visibly before us, to Resolve us friendly, and verily in all such Matters & things, as we shall rationally Desire, and Demand of you, that Amongst the Rest in particular as concerning our recovering and obtaining the treasures, that Lyeth hidden or Buried here or Elsewhere, let the spirit or spirits that hath the Keeping thereof, be Discharged and quitted of It, & immediately in all peace & quietness avoid & Depart therefrom, and Permit & yield up the Same to us as aforesaid: And the Peace of God always Remain Between you & us, in the name of the Father & of the Son and of the holy Ghost, And do for us herein as for the servants of the highest,*

Let the first of these four invocations be observed to be practiced, the first seven nights of the moon's increase, beginning the next night after She Change, as is before taught, and then the Eighth night, beginneth the Latter, & invocate nine times an hour, in the right season, from Eleven of the Clock till two, for that they being most frequently then visible, and stirring about, therefore Most convenient, and opportune, to Call upon them: for God hath So decreed, that they Shall not be visible and frequent in the Day as in the night, Except they are privately Called upon in the Day, because they shall not be frightful nor offensive, to harmless & innocent people, for he hath bounded all things, and they Cannot pass their Limits without permission.

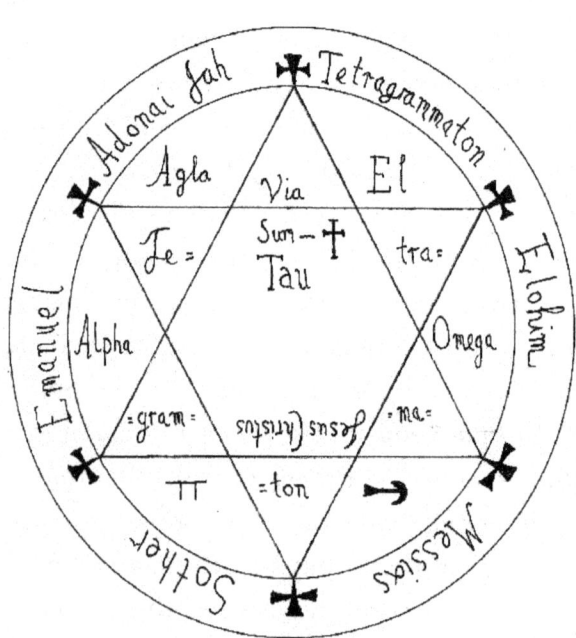

MAGIC CIRCLE FOR FAIRY CONJURATION

Of Types of Treasure & Hauntings

By these Distinctions, a man's Capacity may Easily judge, by what Spirit or spirits, any hidden or Buried Treasures are Kept, be they of what Order so ever, or the Cause, why any house or place is haunted & troubled or infested, which being truly Known, is by patience and perseverance, and a prudent management of Such Affairs, according to this Art And wherein it Is to be Required, to be overcome and vanquished, and the house or place freed from such hauntings, molestations & troubles, of all spirits, Sylphs[93] or Fairies, or any other spirits of what order or nature Soever, whether Aerial, Terrestrial or Infernal, But if the Philosopher[94] Proficient in this art, and other his fraternity, in any matters of this or the Like nature, have neither patience nor prudence, and the master Philosopher, undertaking the management, of what is Requisite to be performed in this art as aforesaid, hath no judgement to Distinguish Between one thing & another in whatsoever goeth about, they May go shoo the Goose.

There are many Castles, old monasteries, and Abbeys and houses, & many other both such like, and, also other places &c: that are haunted & infested With these Kinds of spirits forementioned, the Reasons thereof are more than one

---

[93] Sylphs are specifically mentioned due to their airy nature.
[94] The text reads *'Philosophical'*, but this was probably a copyist's error, as Philosopher makes more sense.

&c: but It is, and always hath been observed, & by practical Experience found, that generally it is for no other Cause or Reason, than that treasures are hidden thereabouts, sometimes It may prove Otherwise, as that some horrid murder hath been committed there, or that some heinous Extraordinary Crimes have been acted, and frequently practiced; by some infernal inclined Caitiff,[95] not caring what wrong &c he did in his life time, who hath Lived there, & died unrepentant, obstinate, persisting to the End, Dying as uncharitably and unworthily, as before he Lived inhumanely & wretchedly: or otherwise some person owning & Living therein, hath been by Such Kind of Hell Hound, persecuted, Chased & Cozened, & foregoing that his Estate must be wasted, & torn from him and his posterity, & that all must come to Ruin & destruction, Layeth these things to heart, falleth Sick & Dyeth in the midst of his Disturbances, & Discontents unreconnected in him Self, & so Do parteth this world in a Distracted condition, leaving nothing behind him amongst his posterity, but Distraction and Destruction.

The Cries whereof Distracteth the Heavens, & passing the Ears of Divine providence Both in all such, and the Like heinous and unpardoned Crimes, the Almighty Being so provoked and offended, permitteth the Executioners of his Justice, to take Vengeance thereon, and punish the place for the Cause Sake. All which Matters, Also, others of the like Nature, is many times much Suspected by some, & Known by others, both neighbours & other Relations, who fancy many times, having An Occasion to be thereabouts late in the night, about some necessary Occasion or other, that they hear some Kind of strange, Dreadful or unusual Noises or

---

[95] A cowardly or despicable person.

Other: or that they see some more than usual Apparition, either in Some Strange frightful shape, or that it was In the very Similitude, or in the very habit of Such a one. when he was Living which if true may be, is a sign & warning to all people, that God taketh notice & vengeance of our Wickedness, but these things very seldom or rarely happen.

Treasure Trove is various & Different in its Recovery or Discovery, which we thus, manifest from the Tradition of the Ancients, setting aside what we have Seen & Known by Experience, both herein And as is aforesaid: We must understand, that the two last Kind of Terrestrial Spirits, next forespoken of, being more humane & Courteous to man, than the Aerial & infernals, by reason of their Sympathy & proximity with him, can & do work, & amongst the rest of their Arts they use, to Coin the Gold and Silver they take out of mines, Into that Country's Coin where they find It, and willingly Dwell & frequent in, which is wherein all places where minerals are (for they love not all places, though their mines Be never So Rich and Royal &c) neither where they are, Do they take away or work upon all, but only a small proportion thereof, So, that still getting a little from Every place, as it groweth & Cometh to maturity, always add to their Store.

Some others Delight to wander & go abroad, & work amongst miners, who also bring home their wages, Some Delight in other trades, and Some to be in Gentlemen's Services, still Like the [...][96] and full Be Bringing all home, and multiplying their treasury, for they are never vile nor Experience, nor will accompany with no one or other person living, in the Common way of Eating & Drinking, though they

---

[96] Unintelligible word.

love them never So well, yet they will work and do any Laborious thing for, and amongst men, but will not accompany them the times when they Eat or Drink.

These Kinds of treasures, are not Easily but with difficulty to be Obtained; Such as hath been made by man & used amongst men, and with less Difficulty obtained And if at any time a magical Philosopher Should Discover Such treasures, as is of their one Manufacture[97], & proceeds to Obtain & get the Same, and though they Seem to yield up and Donate the same to him, yet they will by such Crafts & subtleties, as they are well Knowing in, Convert it to the likeness or Similitude of a Clear Contrary, and baser & most Vile and contemptible matter, as Earth, Clay, Dung, Shards, Soil, or some Kind of Despicable and Regardless matter, or Else to move it; and then is the Philosopher at a loss:

But if any such thing as a transmutation should be perceived or Known, to be either Visibly, or otherwise artificially, or by Discerning Something of a Contrary Species or Nature of the place, where it Lyeth; yet Let it be taken up, and let the fire judge of it, and proceed therein after the same manner, as all metals and minerals Are refined and separated, by such means it will return to the Same Essence it had before:

But in Such Treasures as they, as hath been the Manufacture of and Used amongst men, they Seldom or never Do so by Such Treasures as are not Kept by any Spirit, or that any of these terrestrials should be wandered from, and that Lyeth in some obscure unfrequented place, some person may on a sudden Set or work there And so by near Accident may Discover & carry away the same, without the

---

[97] The word given is *"Manufacturison"*.

Least Knowledge of any thing in this Art, Or otherwise these spirits foreknowing, that such a person will be At such a place, at Such a time, and though they should have the Keeping of the same & leave, Having a great Love & friendship to such a one, or the Like, Do quit the same & leave from him against he Cometh there to work, by reason of which Sudden intended action & intermission, the matter comes to be thus accidentally Discovered and gotten, that otherwise might Lie there many years even time out of mind, or Removed to Another place so never to be Discovered, &c:

Also, such Treasures as are Kept by such Spirits or Terrestrial first before spoken of, as the Executioners of God's Justice Thereupon &c: are not so easily to be found and obtained, as such that are hidden Innocently, Either for future persons or from fear or Danger of a loss, and afterwards happens to be Kept, by the monstrous Sort of Terrestrial Spirits, as Sylphs, Fairies &c: or the Like.

Experiment to obtain Treasure Trove

Choice Experiment How to obtain Treasure Trove

Having a Chamber pretty free or private, from the passage of many people, in a place Indifferent: Airy, being Kept Clean, and Suffumigated with good Odours; write upon an Abortive or on fair Clean Paper, with the Blood of a black Cock as followeth:

Sathan, **Baramper**, **Barbasan**, come with Speed to this place, and bring to me the Treasure: &c: (have set down either the particular thing you invocate for, and the place from whence you would have It brought, or Else a sum certain from Such a place or places, where treasures Lyeth hidden, also Kept from the use of man, for whose Relief it was Originally Decreed and preordained, by the Goodness of the most High and Omnipotent Creator of Heaven & Earth, & all that is in them Contained, as the Sum of 300[98] &c)

Then have a Circle in readiness (made as is hereafter taught) and lay It down on the Chamber floor, and have a little pallet bed at the one End of the Chamber, that hath a full or good sight to the Door, and in a pretty fair starlight Evening, first fix the paper, or Abortive Parchment, whereon is written your Request, with the blood of the black Cock, &

---

[98] This refers to a sum of £300, see later in text. This amount would have been a fortune at the time of writing.

then Enter and so Consequently the Circle, And say the following Conjuration 9 times,

*I Exorcise, Conjure and Constrain thee Spirit **Barbasan**, the spirit of Treasures, by the power and in the name of the Father, and of the Son, & of the Holy Ghost, and by the majesty and Potency of the Omnipotent & Everliving God, **Jehovah**, who made Heaven & Earth, the Sea, & Created all that in them is, and by these his great & Efficacious names, **Agla**, **El**, **On**, **Tetragrammaton**, **Adonay**, **Iskyros**, **Athanatos**, **Paracletus**, **Immortalis**, **Alpha & Omega**, and in the Sacred name of our Lord Jesus Christ the Second person in the Trinity, & in the Godhead and the saviour of the world, who hath given full power & Authority to all that believe, & Lay Hold on him by faith in his name, to adjure & command all spirits of all orders what so ever, whether Aerial, Terrestrial or Infernal, to serve & obey them, whatsoever they shall Command them to Do, in their Several & Respective offices, where they are ordained, and set, by almighty God, and therein to fulfil the Desires & Requests of us, as we are Children & Servants of the Highest,*

*& by those inestimable & unparalleled Miracles, by our Saviour & only mediator, & advocate, Jesus Christ, the High King & Sovereign Lord of all the world, showered Down upon Earth, and by him left to his Apostles and Disciples, and by him to all posterity, that believe by the virtue, power, efficacy and remembrance whereof, I Exorcise, Conjure and powerfully Command the spirit **Barbasan** And more Especially and particularly, by these Great & Sacred names of one god In three persons **Almo**, **Glyas**, **Messias**, **Agios**, **Jesus Christus**, who is was & is to come, & by the High Great & powerful name Egia, which wise Solomon heard in Gabaon, & obtained that Inestimable treasure of wisdom and Riches, By all that is*

before Said, & the great Efficacious and inestimable power, and virtue thereof, thereby Command & Constrain thee **Barbasan**, the which if your Master shall Command you to Do Anything that you may Do, that you Bring to me this night (here nominate your Desires as aforesaid)

And I further Charge & command thee, that in the performance hereof, As thou art bound according to thy orders & office to Do; that thou neither obstruct[99] nor affrighten me, nor any other person, whatsoever, but Quietly and in humility Come, appear & show in a Comely & Decent form and shape, & no ways terrible to me, your Self personally present before me, and Bring along with you the Treasure (rehearsing here again, what is written on the Schedule, Either the treasure from Such or Such a place, if you are certain with thy good Information or otherwise, that such a thing is there mentioning whether It be Gold, Silver, Plate, Jewels, or any matter whatsoever, that was Ordained for the use of man, or Else so nominated to the sum of 300 pounds in Coin), And peaceably Leave It here with me, so that I may enjoy the same for necessary and worthy use, Benefit & Relief.

All which I adjure & Command thee to Do & perform, in all things, particularly and fully, according as I have written & hereby specified, Requested and commanded of you, forthwith immediately without any fraud, loss, hindrance or tarrying, in the name of the Great & Immense **Jehovah** the Almighty & Everliving God, & of his Son Jesus Christ the Great Messiah, & Ever to be glorified Second person in the holy trinity in the Godhead; our only Saviour, advocate and mediator, who shall Come to judge the Quick & the Dead, and the world by fire, In whose name therefore prepare ye & make haste.

---

[99] Word unclear, this is the obvious possibility.

Say this Conjuration nine times Manfully, and with Good faith and Courage & then Say as followeth, and be not Dismayed, for nothing can hurt you, then proceed viz

*I Earnestly request you & Conjure you **Baramper**, that you send your Servant **Barbasan** to me this night, with the Treasure in Such a place, or the Sum of £300 in current Coin & (here also you must mention your Desires, as is before expressed) in nomine Patris & filii & Spiritus Sanctus*

Then betake yourself to your Bed, and about midnight you may perceive the Spirit **Barbasan** will appear in the Chamber, probably in human Shape or form, as in the Similitude of man, or man Kind, and will bring with him that which was invocated for – now if you have a mind to speak to him, before you Licence him to Depart, you may say unto him thus – who are you – he will answer again & Say, I am the spirit **Barbasan**, or to the like purpose, bringing to you the treasure, or such a sum of money accordingly as you have So Earnestly Requested, Then shall you answer again and say unto him as followeth,

*I thank you master **Baramper** and you likewise, and I give you leave & adjure you to depart in peace to your orders, the place of your Residence originally Decreed, & by almighty God appointed for you, And I command you In the name of the Father, & of the Son, & of the Holy Ghost, that you without injuring me nor hurt me, nor anyone upon the face of the Earth whatsoever: wherefore Depart in peace, and let peace be and continue between you & me, in the name of Jesus Christ the high King & Lord of all the world, and I Request and adjure you to be ready to come again to me upon the Like occasion, whensoever & wheresoever I shall call upon you & so you may Depart, & the peace of God remain between us, in nomine Patris & filii & Spiritus Sanctus.*

Then will he Depart, and leave with you that which was Required of him, then at your Leisure you may arise from Bed, and Return thanks to God for the benefits received.

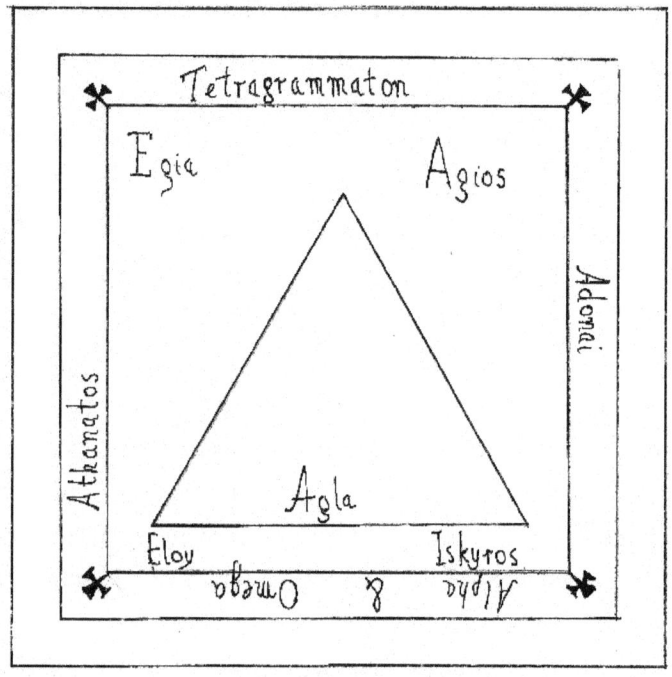

"Magic Circle" for Barbasan

Circles, Triangles, Quadrangles, Pentagonals, Hexagonals, Septagonals, Octagonals, &c: be they, or what form soever they are all Called, Circles of Art, And are all but one & the same In matter & signification, for they are a Fortress or Defence for the Invocant, against Malevolent assault of false appearances Or Evil Illuding spirits, who are many times at hand, to do some Malefices or so to put by the Invocant off his purpose, Which he may perceive if he be Learned Or any way Skillful in this Art, for Being Inviolate on Every Side, with some one or other of the great and Sacred Names of God, Is thereby Defended from any personal

Assault or prejudice, because all spirits, of what Orders Under the Celestial Angels & Intelligences &c: Do Obey them, fear them, & Even tremble At them, So that the Invocant having time & Courage to Speak to them, may be Earnest, Interrogating them to Know, whether the apparition be the Same he Called for, or any other Illusive show; the which his prudence must Direct him.

As for the making of those Circles, for any purpose Or Experiment in this Art, Do thus take your Large Calf Skin parchment, and paste or fasten them together, So that they may be Easily cut or made four squares, on the outside, when they are fastened Or fixed Together, first cutting the insides even where they meet together in the Inwards parts, to be pasted or otherwise fastened together, and then at what time, & in what place Soever, one is minded to invocate, it is but taking up the Circle, roll it up and carry it where occasion & place requires, & So Lay It Down without any trouble, having a loop at Each corner to fasten it to the Ground.

When the four Skins are fastened together and set four Square, then with a pencil & good Ink or Other painting or Colouring matter, Draw the Lines and write the names that are to be written; As in the Example, Then take the Juice of marigold, Vervain and Langue-de-boeuf,[100] and wash the Names that are in the inside of the Circle therewith, And the names of art in the Outward Circle Wash with the Blood of the Black Cock, & then is all Done & made fit for Practice & Action.

---

[100] Ox-tongue.

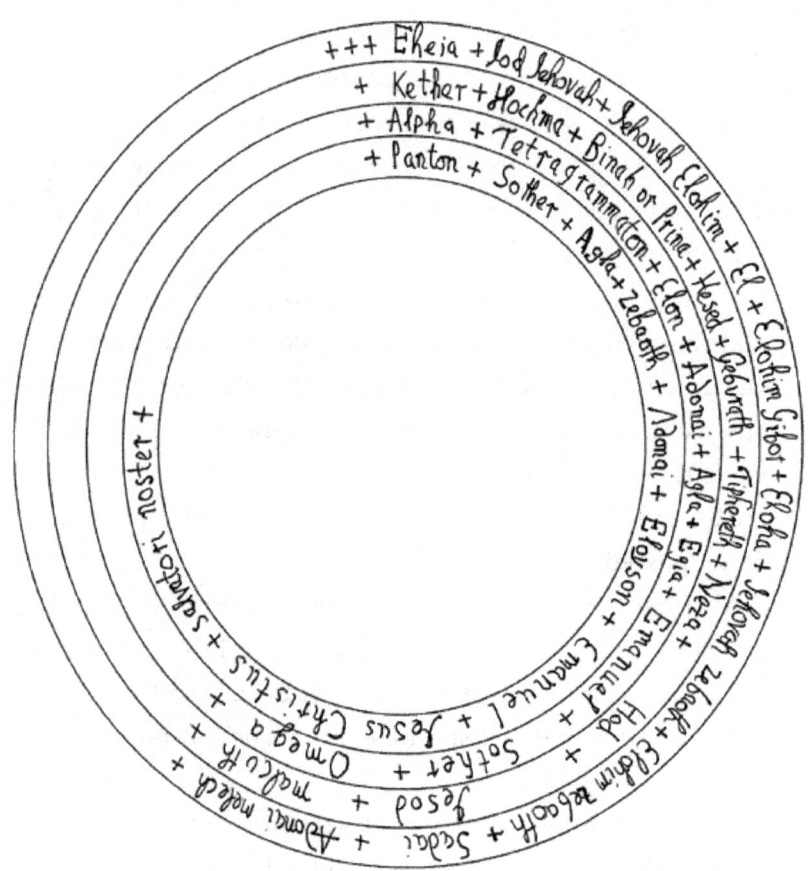

MAGIC CIRCLE FOR TREASURE SPIRIT CONJURATIONS

Experiment with Bret

An Experiment of Bret, A Carrier to fetch Goods from the Sea

When the Moon Is in the Sign Pisces, and well Aspected, and if possible on the Monday or the Thursday, repair to the place appointed for action, Lay down the Circle in Order, the Copy whereof followeth, and the Characters, the Copy of which also followeth adjacent to the Copy of the Circle, fairly written in an Abortive; before the Circle on the Outside, to the East, Invocate as followeth:

I Exorcise & Conjure & Command thee spirit **Brett** *In the name of the father & of the Son & of the Holy Ghost, that thou Do appear Visibly Unto me in fair & human form & similitude of man, & I powerfully Urge & Constrain thee, by & in the mighty Great & Glorious name of God* **Tetragrammaton Jehovah**, *that thou Do for me as for the Servant of the Highest, in the fulfilling of all Such matters & things whatsoever (according to your Orders) as I shall Desire and Request of you,*

And I further and again Exorcise and Conjure the spirit **Brett**, *by & in the names who are powerful & High of our omnipotent & Gracious Lord God:* **Adonay, Sabaoth, Agla, El, Saday, Elohim, Alpha & Omega**, *& by & in the name of our Lord & Saviour Jesus Christ,* **Messias, Sother, Emanuel**, *of wonderful power & Efficacy, at the pronouncing whereof all things ought at their peril, to be Submissive, humble & obedient, by the Virtue whereof I bind Charge and constrain* *thee Spirit **Brett**, to appear Affably, meekly and visibly here before me, in a fair, handsome & human Shape, peaceably, & not frightful nor hurtful to me, or any other person whatsoever; wherefore now prepare ye, make haste & come away, in the name of him who shall come to judge the Quick and the Dead & the world by fire.*

Rehearse this Exorcism Several times, and when he is appeared then bind him with the bond of spirits, and ask him what Questions you please, & he will Certainly answer you, & also if you Command him any Service according to his Orders and office, he will assuredly answer you and obey you, & perform all things In Bringing what he is Enjoined, And when your Desires are fulfilled, then Licence him to Depart, But Detain him not above an hour or two. As for General and Constraining Exorcisms, which are to be used upon occasion in their proper places, and for the Bonds and Licences of Departure of spirits, they are written Elsewhere hereafter, with Directions to use them.

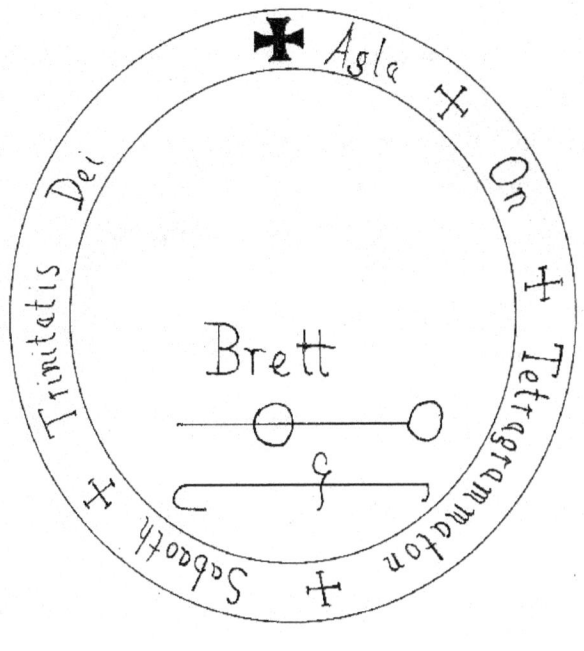

SEAL OF BRETT

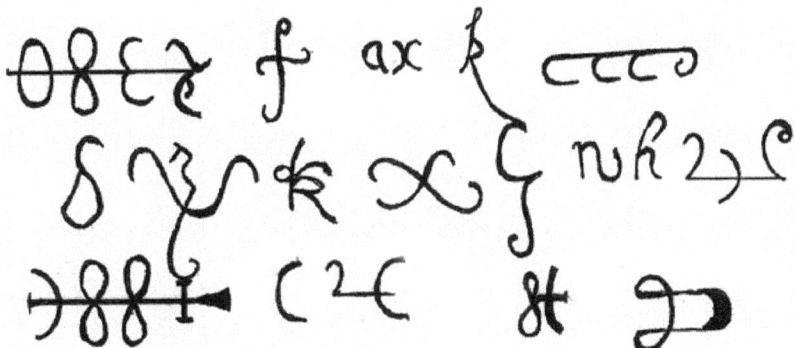

CHARACTERS FOR BRETT

These are the Characters that ought to be placed before the Front on the outside of the Circle, which is where the name **Brett**, And the Character thereto adjoining standeth; the which part must be placed towards the East point of the Compass, and about a foot Distant without, place the above written Characters fairly Inscribed, Either In Virgin parchment or an Abortive.

Conjuration of Birto for King Edward IV

An Experiment of the Spirit Birto as hath often been proved at the Instant Request of Edward the fourth, King of England.[101]

In the Second, fourth, Sixth, tenth or twelfth Days of the moon's Increase, go to the place appointed for this & the like purpose, and in the Evening, when the Air is serene, lay Down the Circles and Character in their Orders (as is hereafter Explained, in the Copies thereof) then Invocate as followeth.

I Exorcise, Call upon & Conjure thee spirit which art Called **Birto***, by the Dignity of thy prince* **Ornotheos** *and* **Booth***, and in the name of the Father & of the Son & of the Holy Ghost, and by the power of those potent, inestimable, Divine and Commanding names, of the almighty & Everliving God* **Jehovah***,* **El***,* **Elohim***,* **Sabaoth***,* **Adonay***,* **Tetragrammaton***,* **Alpha & omega***, and in the name of Jesus of Nazareth, born of a Virgin, the only Begotten Son of God The Father Almighty maker of heaven & Earth, our only Saviour & Redeemer, advocate & mediator, whose name the Celestial Host of Angels honour & obey, and whereat all*

---

[101] An earlier version of this conjuration is in Folger MS Vb 26, and later versions of this may be found in other MSS, e.g. Wellcome MS 3203, John Rylands GB 0133 Eng MS 40.

Knees on Earth do bow, & all the Aerial terrestrial & infernal spirits Do fear & tremble, by all Aforesaid,

*I do yet again powerfully Exorcise, Conjure and Command thee spirit which art Called **Birto**, that thou Do immediately forthwith, and at the present, appear Visibly before me, in that Circle appointed for thee, in fair & human form & shape of a man, and no ways terrible or hurtful to me, or any other person whatsoever & I Constrain thee to tell me the truth and verily, of all such things as I shall Ask & Demand of thee without fraud, guile & Deceit &c: in his name, to whom be all honour, power, Glory & might, majesty & Dominion for Ever & Ever Amen.*

Let the Conjuration be often repeated and said with ample Courage, Confidence & Resolution. And when he is appeared, receive him Courteously & Gently, bind him with the bond of spirits, & then he will freely & faithfully Declare, and make answer to whatsoever shall be Demanded, and will Serve, obey, fulfil all Commands &c: Then Licence him to Depart in peace &c:

CIRCLES AND DRAGON FOR BIRTO CONJURATION

Let the Circle (for the Invocant) which is that wherein the name Magister is written, be made as is before Described, and let the Effigy or Character of the Dragon, or Wyvern be fairly Drawn or painted upon an Abortive; And as for the Circle wherein the spirit **Birto** appeareth it may be made two or three several ways according to the place that is made Choice of to Act in and the Ground or floor: If the Ground be naught & Rugged, as in woods & Copses, as they Generally are, then must the Ground be pressed & made very Even, so that an Impression may be made visible & plain thereon, or let it be made on a large Calf Skin Parchment, but It is far better on the Ground.

And if upon a parchment or floor, then Let it be made or drawn thereon with Chalk or marking stone, and place them three foot asunder, And herein take a serious & Deliberate Consideration, and let Reason & prudence & principle be thy Guide, without which principles, a magician is but a shadow to a substance, and shall as soon miss the height of his Expectations.

Conjuration of Bealpharos

Of the Spirit **Bealpharos** &c:

To invocate, call upon & have Converse with this Spirit Bealpharos, these Rules are to be observed.[102]

On Thursday or Friday in the Increase of the moon, repair to the place appointed for Action, and write on a piece of Virgin parchment, as hereafter followeth in the Copy and write also on a girdle or Thong of a Lions', or a Hart's, or Buck's Skin, also hereafter followeth, with Directions thereunto annexed, and before you Enter the Circle, to Invocate write + **Agla** on the right hand on the left hand these Characters + [✝] ℮ ⅄ ℮ ✝][103] and when you Enter the Circle, make the Sign of the Cross thereon and Say, *Per Crucis hoc Signum fugiat, procul omne malignum: & peridem Signum Salvetur quodque Benignum,* then Invocate as followeth, being Courageous & not at all Dismayed, at first before Invocation, rehearsing the words written on the Breast plate Viz

---

[102] This is previously found in an earlier form in Scot's *Discoverie of Witchcraft* Book XV Ch. XIIIV as An Experiment of Bealphares.

[103] The word is missing, and a gap present in the MSS. The same is also the case in derivative MSS like John Rylands GB 0133 Eng MS 40. However as this is derived from Scot, I have simply added in the markings as given by Scot.

Homo   Saccarus   Muselomeas   Cherubosca

I Exorcise Conjure and Command the Spirit **Bealpharos** *by & in the great name of the Omnipotent and Everliving God,* **Jehovah, Tetragrammaton, Agla, El, On, Jah, Adonay, Saday**; *and by his mighty holy and unspeakable majesty & goodness, and by & in the great Powerful inestimable & inestimable*[104] *names of his only Begotten Son Jesus Christ our Lord, the Redeemer of the world, the Second person in the Trinity, Sitting at the right hand of the Father, the maker of heaven & Earth,* **Messias, Sother, Emanuel, Alpha & Omega**, *& by the true & most Especial names of your master, I do hereby powerfully Exorcise, Command & Constrain thee Spirit* **Belpharos**: *to come & appear Visibly here before us in this Circle in fair & human shape of man or woman Kind, & not terrible by any manner of ways, neither to us nor any other person whatsoever, this Circle being our protection and Defence, through the merciful Goodness our Heavenly God & Loving father,*

I command you to make haste & come away, and show they Self Visibly apparently & peaceably to us here before this Circle, immediately without tarrying or Delay, & with all Humility & obedience, Doing whatsoever I shall Request and Desire of you, without any Illusion, Guile or Deceit, whatsoever, but faithfully truly & certainly to answer, fulfil, & perform Such things as I shall require of you, All which I here powerfully Conjure & constrain you, in the name of him who Said & It was Done, even the most Great & Incomprehensible God, the Creator of Heaven & Earth, who shall Come to judge the Quick & the Dead, & the world by fire.

---

[104] The word *'inestimable'* is repeated here in the text.

This Spirit is somewhat obstinate & pernicious, by nature, and is therefore as usually more slow & prolix In his appearance, wherefore It is Requisite, that the Invocant should persevere herein, with Constancy fervency & patience, & not to Despair at all, though the experiment may prove more tedious than is Expected, for at length he will appear, and his coming is very Sudden, and his motion Is very swift, therefore Let the Exorcist Rehearse the Invocation as oft as he may well do, according as his Reason & prudence shall direct him, as at Every half & Quarter of the Hour whilst he is upon Action, & be very Diligent to Discover his appearance and motion, that he may Immediately Receive him & bind him with the bond of spirits, to stay & abide So long peaceably and obediently with him, in such form & shape, as he shall appoint or approve, until his Demands and Desires be fulfilled, which when done Licence him to Depart: he Resolveth many Dubious Queries, and is also a Carrier as is Spirit of Brett

And with all observed both in this and all other Experiments of Aerial spirits, That as soon as a spirit is bound and is perceived to become obedient & familiar (as by degrees they will) that your Questions & Demands be first Concluded & Resolved on, and fairly written in paper or parchment, that you may have them ready, to propose as occasion shall Require.

That which followeth is to be written on a Girdle, made in Leather or parchment, of the Skin of a Lion or of a hart, and put on by the Invocant before he Entereth the Circle, & so by him to be worn, so long as he is upon Action, **Elie, Elion, Escherie, Deus, Eternus, Eloy, Elemens, Deus sanctus, Sabaoth, Deus Exercituum, Adonay, Deus**

mirabilis, Iao, Verax, Anepheketon, Deus Ineffabilis, Saday, Dominatur Dominus, On Fortissimus, Agla, On, Tetragrammaton, Alpha & Omega.[105]

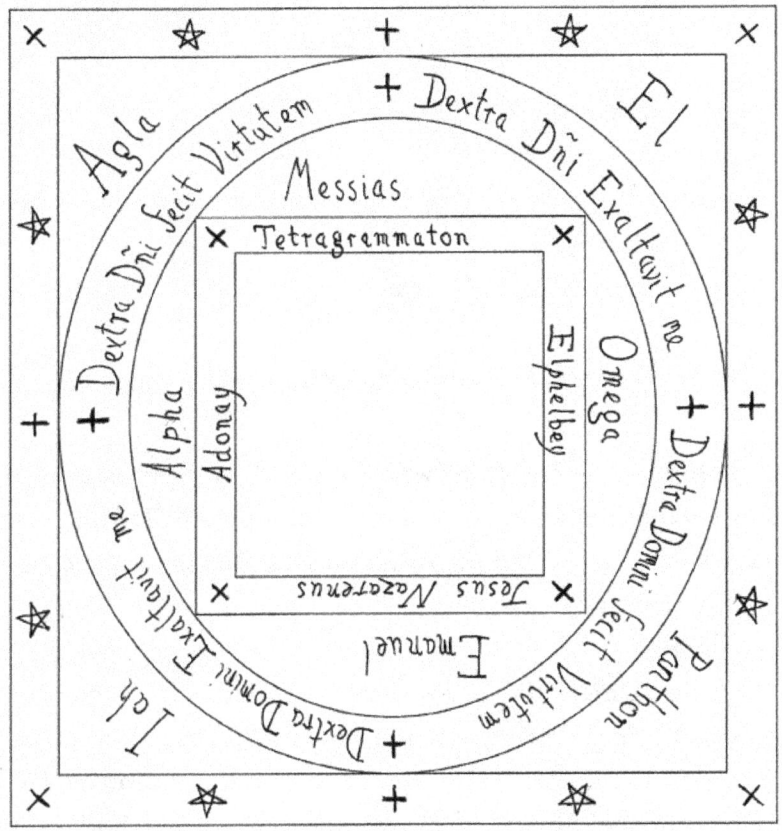

MAGIC CIRCLE FOR BEALPHAROS CONJURATION

THE WORDS IN THE CIRCLE ARE FROM PSALM 117(118):16, "DEXTERA DOMINI FECIT VIRTUTEM, DEXTERA DOMINI EXALTAVIT ME" – "THE RIGHT HAND OF THE LORD HATH WROUGHT STRENGTH, THE RIGHT HAND OF THE LORD HATH EXULTED ME."

---

[105] This is also derived from Scot, from Book XV Ch. XIIIV as An Experiment of Bealphares: + *Helie* + *helyon* + *esseiere* + *Deus æternus* + *eloy* + *clemens* + *heloye* + *Deus sanctus* + *sabaoth* + *Deus exercituum* + *adonay* + *Deus mirabilis* + *iao* + *verax* + *anepheneton* + *Deus ineffabilis* + *sodoy* + *dominator dominus* + *ôn fortissimus* + *Deus* + *qui*. Note the minor changes, and also that Scot was already corrupting text!

LAMEN FOR BEALPHAROS CONJURATION

This Figure must be written in Virgin parchment, and then fixed or fastened on a new piece of Linen Cloth, & worn upon the Breast of the Invocant, During the whole time he is upon Action in the Circle.

This Circle the Invocant Standeth in, when he Invocateth or Calleth upon the spirit **Alpherez**, and it may be made as afore taught, in the Experiment of **Baramper** & it would not be amiss, if the Master Exorcist, had white Vestment or Surpliss[106] on him, And white shoes, and one or two with him in the Circle, only shod with white shoes also.

---

[106] Or Surplice, a sleeveless white linen or cotton tunic reaching to the shins, with slits for the arms to be put through.

Of Evil Spirits

There are a kind of Spirits Subterranean and obverse, which are the Angels that failed, Bringers of Wickedness, according to the Decree of the Divine Justice as they are evil Angels, and wicked Spirits, because many times they annoy and hurt even of their own accord, and there are Legions of them, they are likewise distinguished according to the Names of the Stars, Elements and parts of the World. Of these, four most mischievous Kings[107] do govern and bear rule over the other; according to the four parts of the World, under whom are many more Princes and Governors of Legions governing, and many more of private Offices.

Those kind of Spirits inhabit a place neither airy nigh to the Earth, or within the Earth it Self: There is no mischief which they dare not commit (if God gives them leave). Their Customs are altogether violent and hurtful, and they plot, contrive, & perpetuate many endeavours full of mischief and Disasters. And when they make any Intrusions, Sometimes, they lie hid, and Sometimes do offer open Violence. They are very much delighted in all things done wickedly and Contentiously.[108]

---

[107] This refers to the Demon Princes Paymon, Amaymon, Egin and Oriens. See *The Keys to the Gateway of Magic*, Skinner & Rankine, 2005.

[108] This section has been moved, as in the original it precedes the section on the girdle and interrupts the material about Bealpharos.

Experiment of Vassago

An Experiment of the Spirit Vassago, who may be called upon, to appear In A Crystal Stone, or Glass or Otherwise without.

First, Let the magical Practitioner provide a Lamen or plate of silver, and Engraven upon, according, as is Represented hereafter, and a spatula made of Ash, pear tree, or any other solid wood, the thickness of a third part of an Inch, & the square top thereof to be three Inches square, and the stem, or handle to be nine Inches Long, & gilded all over with Gold, and, the Characters written therein as is showed forth in the example following.

So having all things in Readiness, repair to the Chamber or place appointed for practice, which ought to be Clean, & a Table placed therein, covered with a Clean Linning[109] Cloth, & a taper on Each Side of the Crystal Stone, or Glass, & being stared thereat, Invocate as followeth:[110]

I Exorcise Call upon & Command the spirit **Vassago**, *by & in the name of the Immense and Everliving God* **Jehovah, Adonay, Elohim, Agla, El, On, Tetragrammaton,** *And by &*

---

[109] This is given, though the author possibly meant *'linen'*.

[110] This conjuration is found in the writings of Frederick Hockley. It is interesting to note that a number of the names given here have become corrupt in Hockley's version, suggesting he was copying a copy rather than the original. Waite reproduced Hockley's errors, so he clearly copied his edition from Hockley's copy.

in the name of our Lord & Saviour Jesus Christ, the only Son of the Eternal and true God, Creator of heaven [and earth][111] and All that in them is **Messias, Sother, Emanuel, Primogenitus, Homousion, Bonus, Via, Vita, Veritas, Sapientia, Virtus, Lux, Mediator, Agnus, Rex, pastor, Prophetas, Sacerdos, Athanatos, Paracletus, Alpha & omega**, by all these high, great, glorious, royal & Effable names of the omnipotent God, & of his only Son our Lord & Saviour **Jesus Christ**, the Second person in trinity I Exorcise, command call upon and Conjure thee spirit **Vassago**, wheresoever thou art (East, West, North, or South, or being bound to anyone under the Compass of the Heavens) that you come immediately from the place of your present Residence, And appear to me Visibly in fair & Decent form In that Crystal Stone or Glass, Here, note that the Invocant mentions Crystal or Glass, if he hath one, or Else he Sayeth to me Visibly in fair Decent, and human form, before this Circle &c:

I do again Exorcise & powerfully command the spirit **Vassago**, to come & appear to me in this Crystal stone or Glass, (or otherwise as above) in a fair Seemly And decent form, I do again Strongly bind & Command thee spirit **Vassago** to appear Visibly to me (in that Crystal &c: mentioning as is above Said) By the Virtue & power of these names, by which I can bind all Rebellious obstinate & Refractory Spirits, **Alla, Carital, marital, Carion, Urion, Spylon, Lorean, Stabea, Corian** (or **Coriam**) **mormos, Agion, Cados, Son, Catalon, Yron, Astron, Gardeony, Caldabria, Baon, Tetragrammaton, Strallay, Spyros,**

---

[111] The words *'and earth'* would normally be included here, and the following words *'and all that in them is'* indicate this has been omitted in copying and was the case.

Sother, **Iah**, **On**, **El**, **Elohim** *by all aforesaid, I Charge & command the Spirit Vassago, to make haste & Come away and appear Visibly to me (as aforesaid) without any further or longer tarrying or Delay, in the name of him who shall Come to judge the Quick & the Dead, and the world by fire Amen.*

This Conjuration often Repeated, and the Invocant being patient and Constant in his perseverance, and not Disheartened or Dismayed, by Reason of any tedious Prolixity or Delays, he will at last appear, though It may be Long first of when he is appeared, bind him with the bond of spirits, & then you may talk with him on that this is a true Experiment, & that this spirit hath been obliged to the fellowship & service of a magick Art as heretofore, is very certain, as may appear by this following obligation the which the Invocant may if he pleaseth, have fairly written in an Abortive, And Laid before him, & Discourse with the spirit Concerning It.

A Bond or Obligation of the Spirit Vassago, made to one T.W.

I **Vassago** *Under* **Baro** *the King of the West, not Compelled by Command or fear, but on my own accord & free will, Especially oblige my Self by those present, firmly, faithfully & without Deceit, to T.W.*[112] *to obey at any time, & at any place whensoever, & wheresoever he shall call upon me, personally to appear, whether in a Stone, or in the middle without a Stone, & to fulfil his Commands truly in all things, wherein I can, by the Virtue of all the names of God, & Especially by these words, the most powerful in the Magical Art,* **Lay**, **Alzyrn**, **Mura**, **Syron**, **Walgava**, **Ryshin**,

---

[112] The initials of the magician.

Layaganum, Layarasin, Laysai: *and by the Virtue wherewith the Sun and moon were Darkened, and any planet, and by the Circles & Characters thereof, & primarily by his Seal, binding most Solidly, In witness of which guilty person So Commanding I have Signed this present obligation with mine one Seal to which I always stick close.*

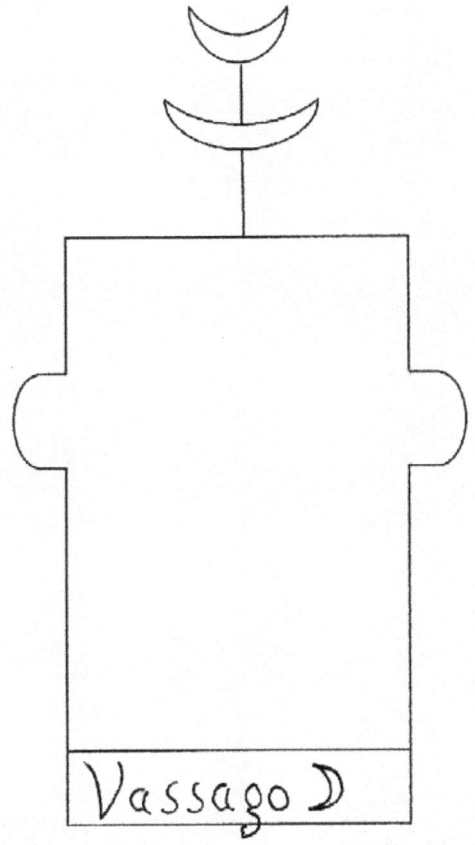

THE SEAL OF THE SPIRIT VASSAGO

That this is a true Experiment is apparent; And that this Spirit hath been by the great Diligence & Constant perseverance of Learned & intelligible Magicians, brought to obedience And fellowship is manifestly true, by this here recited Precedent, besides what my Self hath seen.

And as for the Calling upon this & the Other following spirits, Either in the crystal Stone or Glass, shall be showed at the End of the next Experiment, because they are both of one Nature.

Experiment of Agares

An Experiment of the Spirit Agares

The Experiment and Invocating of this spirit **Agares**, is practically the same as in the former Experiment of the spirit **Vassago**, who Likewise may be called to appear, Either In a Crystal Stone, or Glass, or otherwise without them, and they Are both very slow in their appearance, as most Aerial spirits are, but when once they do appear, then afterwards they will frequently come as the Master Invocates. Having all things In Readiness, and Resolved upon his time, Let him Enter his Chamber Or place appointed for Action, and Invocate as followeth.

Thou Spirit **Agares** *the first Captain under the King of the East, I Exorcise, Command & call upon thee, & Constrain thee by calling, in the name of the most Strong, powerful, fearful, and Blessed* **Jah, Adonay, Elohim, Saday, Saday, Eja, Eja, Eja, Alarie, Alarie,** *& in the name of* **Adonay**, *the God of Israel, who by his immediate word alone, Created the Heavens, the Earth, the Seas, & all things therein Contained, and made man according to the Similitude of himself, and these most Efficacious, powerful & Commanding, ineffable & Sacred Names, of the All powerful and immense God,* **Jehovah Agla, El, On, Tetragrammaton,** *wherein All visions, & apparitions are wont to be, & by the holy name which was written on the Brow of Aaron the priest, of the most High & Everliving God, I powerfully Exorcise & Command thee spirit* **Agares**, *that wheresoever thou art, in* *any place or part of the Air or Earth, East, West, North, or South, or being bound to Any one, that immediately without tarrying or Delay, you presently appear to me Visibly, in fair & human form,*

Here you are to observe, that if you call him with a stone or glass, then you are to say *"In this Stone or Glass"*. If you have none you need not specify but say *"to me"* or *"to me before this Circle"* &c, and to the like elsewhere in other places of this Conjuration, observe the same where you shall meet with the like occasion.

Moreover & again, I Exorcise potently & Command, and call upon the spirit, by him that was Is & shall be, Ever & in the Blessed & great name of the holy & Heavenly Messiah, or Lord & Saviour **Jesus Christ**, *born of a virgin, Lord of all the world, and Its only mediator & Advocate, to the Father of all mercies, & God of all Consolation, at whose great Glorious & incomparable name, all Knees ought to bow, and humbly Do Reverence, and at all the naming whereof all spirits whatsoever, both Aerial Terrestrial & infernal, ought to obey with all Due reverence & submission, who Is the great* **Emanuel** *the faithful witness & primogenitus,* **Alpha & Omega**, *who Lived & was Dead & Liveth forever, & by his glorious passion, Resurrection, & Ascension, & by the Coming of the holy Ghost, by all aforesaid, I powerfully Exorcise, Urge & constrain thee Spirit* **Agares**, *that without tarrying or further Delay, you do now appear Visibly to me, I now Calling upon you, Here mentioning As followeth before, Either within or without the Due place in fair, Solid, decent & human form, wherefore make haste Come away, and show thy self Immediately, to fulfil all my Request, in the name of the Father & of the Son & of the holy Ghost Amen.*

Now if this spirit does not appear, in Some material Distance of time to the Conjuration, wonder not at its prolixity, for (as is Said Elsewhere before) it is the nature of the Aerial Spirits, to be very Slow In their appearances, therefore Let the magician be Constant in his perseverance and prosecution herein, that the experiment is also true, and that the spirit **Agares** hath been called upon, and been brought to obedience and familiar Association, is manifestly true and apparent by this following obligation, made by him to some Learned master.

*I **Agares**, the first Captain under the King of the East, not Compelled by Command or Dread, but willingly and on my own accord, do Especially bind my Self by these Psents,*[113] *firmly, to Obey at all times & in Every place I:M:*[114] *to Do his Command In all things, appertaining to my Duty, & Especially by these words, the most powerful In this Magick Art, **Lay**, **Alyzm**, **Mura**, **Syron**, **Walgava**, **Ryshin**, **Layganum**, **Layarazin**, **Lasai**: And by that Virtue wherewith the Sun & moon were Darkened, before that terrible Day of the Lord (as in the Gospel) and shall be turned into Blood, And by the head of my Prince, & by his Circles & Characters: and Chiefly by this Seal firmly binding, In Witness of which Guilty Person, I have Signed this Obligation, with mine one Seal the Commanding one, to which I Always Stick Close.*[115]

---

[113] Present, an old abbreviation.

[114] The name of the magician, here the person's name would obviously be substituted.

[115] As there is also a Spirit Contract to Padiel in Sloane MS 3824, there are more spirit contracts in this work than in other grimoires.

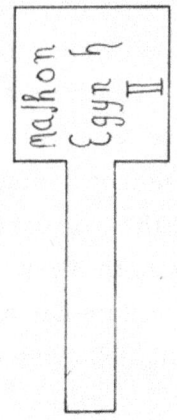

THE SPATULA

The form of the Spatula which ought to be made of any Solid wood handsomely not too thick, and Gilded over & writ upon as here is showed, This spatula serveth for a Sceptre & Signifeth: Dignity Power &c: the which is one main Principle for magick, & is a Type of majesty In Action, Let It be gilt over with Gold.

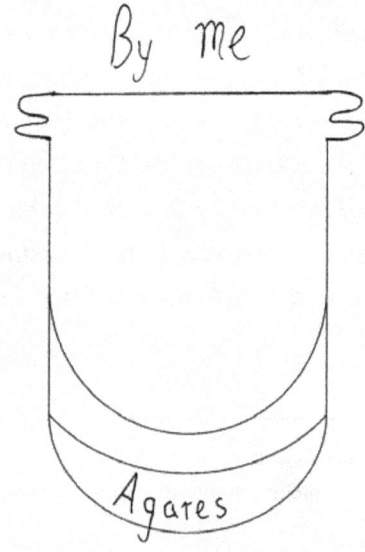

SEAL OF AGARES

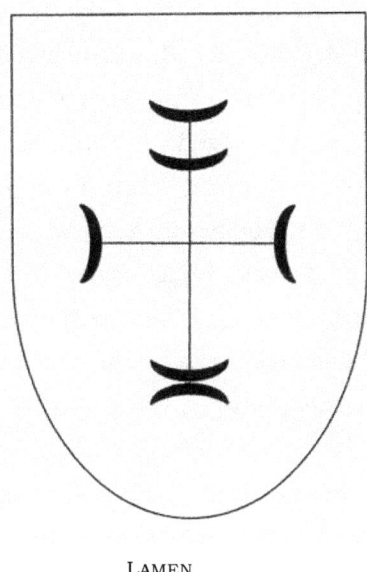

LAMEN

The form of the Lamen, or Sigil, which ought to be made in a plate of Silver, and the figure Engraven thereon as Is here Represented, which sigil must be Hung about the Neck or fixed on the Breast of the Magician, And when he Goeth upon Action Let him Do thus –

If he calleth Either of these two forerecited spirits, Vassago or Agares to appear In a Stone or Glass, then let him set the stone or Glass on the Table in his Chamber of Practice, covered with Clean Linen, and on the side of the Crystal Stone or Glass, to stand a white wax Candle or Else at Leastwise one just behind It, Then Let the magician fix the Silver Sigil on his Breast, and take the Spatula in his Right hand, and seat him self at the table Just against the Stone, & his Companions by him if he hath any, and when he is seated, then he may Either Lay the spatula Down on the table, just before the Stone, or Else hold It in his hand, Even as best pleaseth him self, and let him have his Desires written fairly Down and Laid on the table on his left hand, Just beside the Spatula, & if he pleaseth also the Copy of the obligation Fairly written, In an abortive, with the Seal of the spirit, thereto as is showed In the Copy thereof foregoing, Laid on the Table on his Right hand just on the Other side of the spatula, And so proceed to Action.

But if the Magick Philosopher goeth upon Either of these two Experiments, or Invocateth either of those two last recited spirits **Vassago** or **Agares**, without Either a Crystal Stone or Glass, then when he Entereth his Chamber or place Appointed for Action for practise, Enter the Circle, in form and manner aforesaid Holding the spatula in his right hand or Laying It Down just before him in the Circle, & if he have two Companions, let him on the Left hand hold the Copy of the Demands, and him on the right hand the Copy of the obligation, And so let him proceed to action, and Exorcise manfully, Constantly & firm Resolution. If he useth a Crystal Stone, It ought to be about the bigness of a goose Egg, it matter not whether It be round or oval and to be Set on a frame, which may be done by a jeweller, with a Ring of flat wire, or narrow plate about It, at the bottom whereof Let It be fastened, a Stem of indifferent Length, as the handle of a beer bowl, with a ponderous or heavy pedestal or foot to It, that may stand firm & steady, & then hath he a Complete Receptacle;

CRYSTAL BALL ON BASE

And if the Magick Philosopher maketh a Choice of a Glass Receptacle, he may have It made at the Glass house of Good white Crystal withal, but It Cannot be made Solid as is a stone, but It may be made pretty thick and with a Little Small hole at the top, according as Is here represented, In the Annexed Figure. It is also to be Observed, in the making of this Receptacle of Glass, That the head being made as thick as possible, The Glass maker can make It, It will be pretty heavy, therefore the foot thereof ought to be made pretty broad, & of an indifferent Large Diameter, because of standing the more steady all which Is Easy Enough to be understood.

Hic Est Circulus Experimenti[116]

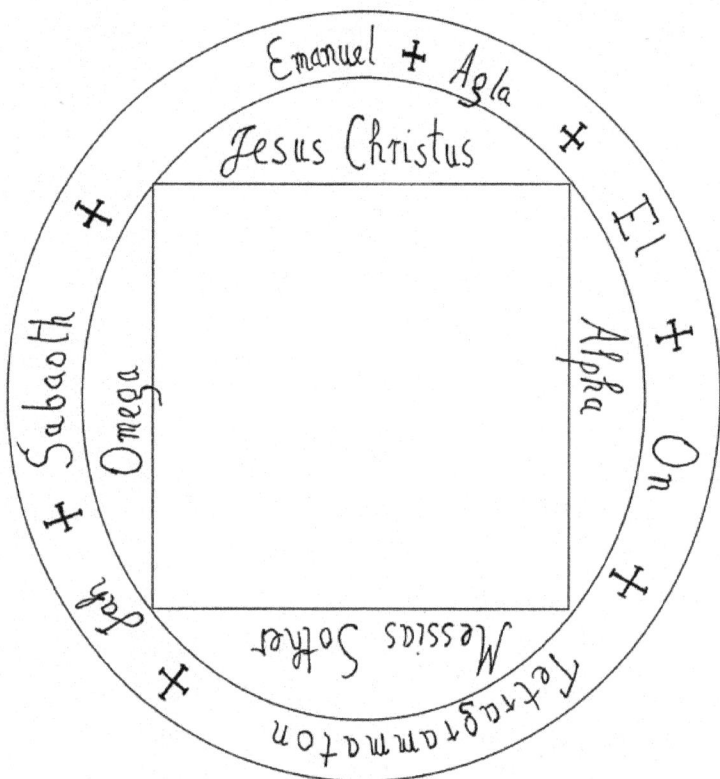

MAGIC CIRCLE FOR VASSAGO OR AGARES

This Circle Serveth for the Invocant to stand in, when he calleth upon Either of the two forementioned Spirits Vassago or Agares, when he Calleth upon them to appear, without Either a Stone or Glass or other Receptacle, So that in Either of these Experiments, he may use his own Discretion, Which the practical part hereof is already before so Clearly Explained, of the which we ourselves have had some Signal Experience.

---

[116] *"Here is the Circle of the Experiment".*

An Experiment to Obtain Your Desire

An Experiment to Obtain Whatsoever is Desired

Take a Lapwing & Let Its Blood In a Glass, wherewith make the Ensign or Square, commonly Called a Circle, though improperly by reason of the Contrary Similitude, but they are Generally Called Circles in the Art, because they all Signify one & the same thing &c: upon four large Calf skin parchments, fastened Evenly & handsomely together, according to Art, as is before taught, And also with the Blood of the Lapwing, write upon an Abortive thus as followeth,

Bolda, Suspensas, in Aeternitas, apar, za, Implant, Dantilion, Avaurion, Fons, Floris, de, Sada, Baldachia, Sarranis, Mars

Let this be written in a Chamber, that is very private and Close shut for the present time, And when these things are Done, & Kept in a Readiness for use then, seek out for a place fit to Do this Experiment In, which must be in an Orchard, or a wood that is Very private,[117] and free from the Passages or oversight of people, the which Being found, than at the time appointed to go upon action, Let the Magical Philosopher having a fair bright sword in his hand, as soon

---

[117] The insistence on trees for the surrounding is an interesting requirement.

as he is Entered into the Orchard or wood, Kneel down on his Knees, and with an Earnest meekness, say what is written in the abortive, three times over; then Let him rise, & having made Choice of the private place that can be found, go thereto, & place this Circle, and with his sword in his right hand, and the Schedule in the left hand, enter the Circle and turning his face to the East, Read the schedule over as oft as is convenient, And at length will appear a vision, like to a fair Knight on horseback, with a Goshawk on his fist,[118] and he will say unto you, Why call you me, What will you Ask, Lo I am here to fulfil all your Requirements

But answer him nothing at all And then turning to face from him to the north, behold him not then will he pass by & vanish, then towards the north proceed as before you did towards the East, and anon will another Vision appear, like a Comely fair Knight on horseback, with a Goshawk also on his fist, riding as it were towards you upon a very Goodly Steed, and he will speak to you Even the like Language, or to the Same effect, as the first apparition, but Say nothing to him, neither give him Answer, and turning to face to the west behold him not, So he will pass away by & Vanish. Then towards the West, observe to Do as before in the East, and North, & presently will a third apparition appear, Like as a goodly Knight on horseback with a Goshawk also on his fist more fair and beautiful than the two former, Crowned with a Diadem of Gold, who will say thus unto you, or much like to it, I am here, and ready for Labour all, for tell me what thou wouldst I do For thee

---

[118] This description could indicate Agares or his servants, as he is the one spirit described in the *Goetia* with a goshawk on his fist.

And this Knight you may faithfully trust, and Desire of him what you will, he will truly fulfil your requests, which you ought to have in readiness fairly written &c: Then will he say, Even as soon as he hath said the former words thus to you: Will you have my fellowship But you Shall Deny It, and answer him saying No you will not, but propose your Desires and Demands to him, what it is you would have him Do for you, and turn your Countenance or face towards the South, and so leave him then shall he pass away from you, and so give over, and Cease Action, & go your way.

The next morning go again to the same place, and there you shall find all your Requests fulfilled, and your Expectations answered, for which give thanks & Depart.

Hic est Quadra: Circulus Experimenti

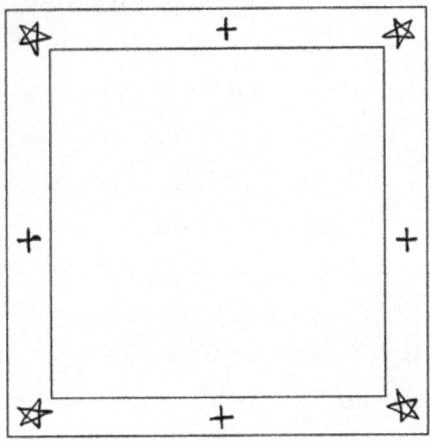

"Magic Circle" for this Experiment

This ought to be written with the blood of the Lapwing upon a fair Calf Skin parchment, neatly & Evenly fastened together, & so made one square Entire thing, & so Kept for practice.

Experiment of Bleth

Of the Spirit Bleth,[119] Who is mostly called upon and appeareth in a glass of water

Have a glass made of pure white metal pretty thick, made in the form of a Urinal,[120] and make a cover thereto of Virgin Wax or parchment with the Character made thereon as hereafter followeth, then fill the glass a little above half full of water, and Set it upon the table of practice, or other Convenient place, where It may stand very Sure and Steady, from Shaking or jogging & let it stand on your left hand and set the Cover thereof by it on the right hand &c: Let the table or place which the Glass and Its Cover standeth, be Covered with a Linen Cloth very white: and so when all things are decently Set in Order, Invocate as followeth:[121]

*I adjure & call upon command and constrain thee O thou spirit which art called **Bleth**: in & through the name of the father & of the Son & of the holy Ghost, Three persons in trinity, & one God in Unity, & by this incomprehensible name, of the most High and Omnipotent Creator of Heaven & Earth,* ***Tetragrammaton, Jehovah****, I powerfully and Earnestly urge and Constrain thee O thou spirit **Bleth** and I call upon &*

---

[119] This is probably the Goetic spirit Bileth.

[120] Yes, it does say that!

[121] This practice resembles the use of bowls of water for containing demons found in early Jewish texts, such as the writings of Flavius Josephus (1st century CE).

command thee to appear Visibly & affably Unto me in this Glass of water, set here before me, as a fit and appointed Receptacle to Entertain you, And I do again adjure Call upon, bind, command and Constrain thee O thou spirit **Bleth**, by the Virtue and might of those Great & powerful names By which Wise Solomon bound spirits, and shut them up **Elbrach, Ebanher, Gosh, Ioth, Agla, Oshie, Venoch, Nabrat**, to appear & show thy Self, fairly & fully and plainly Visible unto me, In that Glass of water here before me, which I have Set to Receive you in and to resolve & openly & manifestly to show me, the Truth Verity & Certainty of all Such matters & things, as I shall Demand & Request of you, without any fraud guile Dissimilation, or other Crafty or Deceitful Illusion whatsoever, wherefore I now call upon & Constrain thee hereby, O thou Spirit **Bleth** in and through these high & potent names of our Lord & Saviour **Jesus Christ, Messias, Sother, Emanuel, Alpha & Omega**, to move appear & show thy self plainly unto me, & fulfil my Demands, desires & Requests in all things, according to your Office, wherein you may or Can without any further tarrying or Delay, but immediately prepare you & come away, and Do for me as for the Servant of the Highest.

Speak this Conjuration often, and when the water Stirreth a Little, & a Smoke Seemeth to be seen In the Glass, then Doth the spirit Enter, for this is the foreshowing Sign of his appearance, & when this is perspicuously Discerned, then Lightly Cover the Glass with the Cover, & bind it all about So Severely, that nothing may Go out &c: Then Ask what you will, & he will either Resolve it viva voce, or it will be seen written on his Breast.

The Spirit **Sonoryan** may be Invocated & called upon, As Either of the foregoing Spirits **Vassago Agares** or **Bleth**, being Exemplary alike, only Changing the name In the Invocation, Some use oil in the Glass instead of water, for so did Cardinal Richlieu, who this spirit **Sonoryan** was very familiar, frequent & Conversant withal &c.[122]

This Character is to be made on the Cover of the Glass

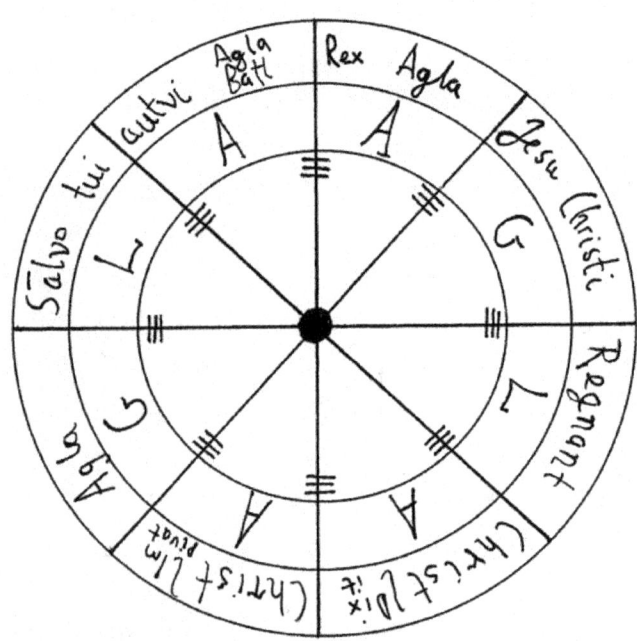

SEAL FOR GLASS

---

[122] This is an interesting claim, for which there is however no supporting evidence!

158 | The Book of Treasure Spirits

Of the spirit **Mamon** & his characters

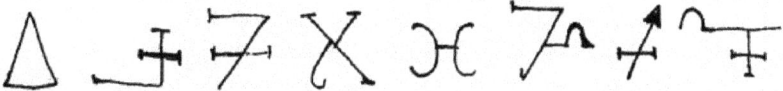

Let these Characters be written in the right hand, with the blood of a Lapwing, or of a black Cat, & when the Spirit is Invocated or called up the Hand must be held up so it may see them.

This spirit together with those that follow, may be Invocated and called up As the foregoing spirits **Vassago** and **Agares** are, the same method being Observed; only the Characters, and names are Altered in the Call or invocation And the practical part of the Experiment

Of the Spirit **Seere** His Character nature & Office &c

This Spirit **Seere** is under the King of the East, He goes & comes & brings all things to sudden and Expeditious effects, He can Carry & recarry, & pass over the whole world, in a moment, yea in the twinkling of an Eye, He makes true Relation of all Sorts of Thefts, & of treasure trove, & shows the true Relations of many other things. He is by nature indifferent, Good, mild courteous and affable, & willingly performs whatsoever is Desired of him &c.

Of the Spirit **Asmodiah** his Character

This spirit showeth all things that are in the Earth and Water, & all things that appertain to Love & marriage, and what shall befall those that be newly married, and show friends, Kindred or Allies, And oft show agreement or Disagreement, & how fate will smile or frown upon them, he can also discover thieves & theft, Treasure Trove & many other notable Occult things.

Of the Spirit **Dantalion** His Character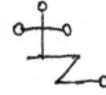

He showeth all arts and sciences, & maketh one Expert therein, he can Declare & reveal the secret councils of anyone, he changeth the minds & thoughts of men & women, he can stir up Love, and show by Vision the similitude of any one, be they at never so great a Distance, in any part of the world &c.

Of the Spirit **Andromalius** His Character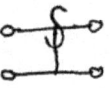

He can bring back thieves with the Goods they have stolen, He discovereth all Manner of Wickedness, & all manner of secrets, Clandestine, underhand dealings, Plots, Contrivances and all deceitful designs, Combinations, Consultations or other Treachery whatsoever tending to the Ensnaring, Detriment, Loss or Destruction of one; & punisheth all manner of Lewd, Slavish, Deceitful, ungodly persons &c: He faithfully declareth the Verity of treasure Trove.

Of the Spirit **Sondama**, alias **Sondanna**

This Spirit was the servant and familiar to Mr E.K. Harppereth In many forms, & then at length in a triangle of fire: but being Constrained to the Circle, he at Last taketh to the similitude (as it was) of a great Giant, and will declare before, for a month to come, what spirits to Orderly Range, such by name being called, will do their offices, &c: this is worth the Consideration & practice Anno: 1500

Of the Demon Rulers

There are many spirits, that are said to be by nature Evil, & not only Envious & Enemies to man & his felicity, but adverse to all goodness whatsoever: and yet have been by magicians of former times (Living in Remote & far Countries from us in England and these parts) brought to a Communication, and a Kind of familiarity, with them, whereby their offices & natures have been Discovered, but it hath not been Common among men, Especially the meanest Capacities, & therefore not at all practiced, neither is it fit to be practiced by any Sober philosopher, unless to Satisfy his Curiosity, because of their Turbulence, But yet they are many times called upon, to bind & constrain other Spirits, to Do their offices, which is not at all offensive hurtful or obnoxious, therefore they may be Invocated in Such cases &c: we shall mention Some thereof, because of Discerning the Difference thereof, & therein let the magick Philosopher use his Discretion &c: There are three spirits Called Devils, or infernal spirits, whose names are mentioned in holy writ, namely **Lucifer**, **Beelzebub**, & **Sathan**, therefore as they stand recorded in the Sacred Scriptures, we shall hint at something of them, & no more.

Lucifer is a great spirit, and may not be Invocated nor Called from his Orders, yet by him as by **Tantavalerion** other spirits may be adjured and bound, for all sprits that are by nature evil, or at least more malign, than usually many Aerial & Terrestrial powers are, such are treated of before, do with a Kind of majesty, Worship & obey him: for this Reason he many not be called upon, Except to Constrain other Subservient spirits to fulfil the Commands & Requests of the Invocant in any Reasonable thing.

The next is **Beelzebub** who is a great prince (and it is said that before the fall, he was of the order of Cherubims) and 1000000 spirits do minister unto him. He appeareth very beautiful, & giveth to them that call him Gold & Silver and maketh them Expert in Science, he appeareth well for half an hour: & giveth to Each Demand a true Answer, He giveth a servant or Familiar, which will be faithful & obedient, During a man's Life, whoso Calleth him must have Tears of Amber, Lignum Aloes mastic &c: & invocate towards the east, in Verbis Conceptis wherein he must be importunately and Earnestly Urged, to Do his office, who then at Length will obey.

The third spirit is called **Sathan**, who was before his fall of the order of Cherubims, & it is Said that because he fell not of his own will, therefore he abideth obscurely in the Air, and so is called the prince of the Air, under whom are four Princes or Kings, bearing Rule in the Air, & have power given & permitted them, to coruscate and Disturb the Air, whereby many Mischiefs befall the Earth, Doing great hurt, and it was this spirit that tempted our forefathers in the Wilderness to Disobedience.

The four Kings of the Air Ruling under **Sathan**, together with their Councillors & messengers are named as followeth, under whom again are numberless of subservients.

Oriens King of the East, appeareth with an hundred & two hundred Legions, having a fair Effeminate Countenance, & a goodly Crown upon his head, riding upon an Elephant, having trumpets, Shalms[123] & much Minstrels of Diverse Instruments going before him, & when he is called he Cometh with other great Kings; but if he be called, alone, then he appeareth in the very likeness of a Royal Horse; He telleth the truth of all things present, past & to Come; giveth money, teacheth Sciences, Confereth Books, and willingly giveth answers to all Demands & Questions, He knoweth all Experiments, and hath power to teach them;

	East		Oriens	Presidential Councillors are	Neophryn, Barbas, Sobarbas, Alilgon, Gordonizor Lamo, Vassago, Othry, Um, Anaboth, Alicho, Berith[124], Mala
King of the	West	is	Paymon	whose	
	North		Egyn	Messengers are	Baal, Temel, Belfarto (or Belferit), Balferth, Belial, Baroson, Rombulence ([125]or Ramblane), Alphasis, Emlon, Ocarbidaton, Madicon
	South		Amaymon		

---

[123] An early woodwind instrument with a double reed, an early oboe.
[124] Berith appears as a Spirit of Earth in *Magia Naturalis et Innaturalis*, 1505.
[125] Romulon appears in Folger MS Vb 26, the probable source of Rombulence

There is a King under **Oriens**, whose name is **Baal**, whose office is to teach all manner of Sciences, and maketh a man to go Invisible, & hath under him 250 Legions, who so acteth by this Royal Spirit **Oriens**, must direct his Countenance & actions towards the east, and at the first Constrain the spirit Temel, who is messenger of the East as followeth – first invocating for the aid and Assistance of **Oriens**, &c: of which Invocation an example hereafter followeth in the practice of Hochma.[126]

*O thou spirit who art called **Temel**, Messenger of the east, I adjure, call upon, bind, command and Constrain thee, by the power, Dignity & authority of the Great and Royal Prince **Oriens**, the supreme Head of your Hierarchy, I adjure, Command, constrain & in the name, & by the Supremacy of your Orders, I powerfully & Earnestly Urge thee, O thou spirit **Temel**, Messenger of the East, to appear & show thy self Visible, affable, and in all mildness & serenity here before us, & in no wise turbulent, hurtful or terrible unto us, or any other Creature whatsoever, upon the Earth, but come ye peaceably, Quickly & in all plainness & humility, & give me true & faithful Answers and Resolves, readily and willingly, of my demands & desires, courteously fulfilling my Request, in all things (according to your Order & office) without Delay, fraud, illusion or other deceitful crafts or impositions whatsoever, that may in any wise so hinder, oppose or obstruct my Expectations in the Least, move therefore.*

---

[126] I.e. wisdom, the name of the second Sephira on the Qabalistic Tree of Life.

This Conjuration being Repeated nine times, and if he appeareth not, then proceed with the Conjuration following, & Rehearse It several times; and herein Act with Care & order, by returning again, to that above, & then again to this below, according to discretion.

O you spirit, **Belfarto** *or* **Belferit**, *who art the messenger of the King of the East, I Exorcise, adjure, bind, Command and Constrain thee, in and through the name of our almighty and Heavenly God, creator of heaven & Earth, & of his only begotten Son Jesus Christ, born of the Virgin Mary, the Redeemer of the World, & our only Mediator & advocate with the Father, of all power mercy & goodness, in whose names all the choir of Celestial Angels Rejoice, before whom they Incessantly Sing,* **O mappa laman Hallelujah**, *and at whose names all Knees upon Earth Do bow, and all the Aerial Terrestrial and Infernal Host of spirits Do fear & tremble, wherefore I do again adjure, bind, command & Constrain you, O you spirit* **Belfarto**, *or* **Belferit**, *and I also potently and powerfully urge & Enforce you, in the name, and by the Dignity and Authority of your prince* **Oriens**, *and the head of your Hierarchy & orders, that now presently, and without tarrying or delay, that you Enforce the Same spirit, which is called* **Temel**, *to appear Visibly, affably and peaceably here before me, and no ways Turbulent, hurtful or terrible to me, or any other creature, and that he may faithfully, humbly, obediently, readily and willingly Do my Commandment and fulfil my Desires in all things, according to his office, wherein he may obey without any test, hindrance, tarrying, tarrying, delay, illusion, fraud, or any other Crafty Deceits or Devices whatsoever, that may oppose, obstruct or deceive me, in my present & future expectations; all which I Constrain and*

Command thee, O thou Spirit **Belfarto**, or **Belferit**, in & through in & through the mighty & binding name **Tetragrammaton, Jehovah**, &c:

Amaymon is a King of the South, He is great & mighty, and appeareth in the Similitude of an old man, with a great Bear; His hair like to horse hair, & hath a bright Crown on his head, and Rideth on a fierce Lion, usually roaring at the first appearance; and shaking a Rod in his hands, his ministering spirits going before him, with all manner of musical Instruments, with him Cometh other three Kings, who are **Emlon, Ocarbidaton**, and **Madicon**, being messengers to the King of the South, he cometh with a great Company and very obscurely &c: He giveth a true Answer to all Demands, & maketh a man wonderful Cunning and deport, in all Learning, Philosophy & Ars Notoria, he giveth the best acquaintance with nobility, & Confirmeth the Doings thereof (as Dignity, promotion, &c: he may be detained one hour: &c: and but no Longer &c: And when you go to act by this spirit **Amaymon**, Direct your Self & Countenance to the South, first Invocating & Constraining the spirit **Emlon**, after the same manner as is before Explained, in the Constraint of the spiritual messengers of the East, under **Oriens** (viz) **Temel** and **Belfarto**, using the same Invocations, only alternating the spirit's names, and then adjuring the other Spirits, **Ocarbidaton** and **Madicon**, as before.

Paimon is King of the West, he appeareth at first somewhat terrible & speaketh with a Hoarse Voice, but being Constrained by a Divine Power, he then taketh the form of a Soldier, and when he Cometh to the presence of the Invocant, is oft times apt to Cavill & make variance, He Rideth upon a dromedary, or a Camel, which is Crowned with a Bright crown, & hath the Countenance of a woman, before goeth a Band of ministering spirits, with all Kind of musical Instruments, And when he appeareth, Let the Invocant Cast a paper to him, wherein is Inscribed, that he shall speak plainly & Distinctly, so that the Master may Understand what he sayeth, And with him Cometh five other principal or regal Spirits, who are **Balserth** the messenger to the King of the west, and **Belial** a King, And **Baroson**[127] a King, and **Rombulence** or, **Ramblane**, and **Alphasis**, they may appear from the 8th hour to the 12th &c: It is also here to be observed, that the spirit **Alphasis**, is first to be Called upon, and Constrained by Invocation, as is to be understood before in the first **Temel**, and then, and then afterwards the Regal Spirits **Belial**, **Baroson**, **Rombulence**, Or **Ramblane**, according to the example of the spirit **Belfarto**, before Recited.

Egyn is King of the North, he appeareth in the Likeness of a man, his face very fair and Clear, his nostrils Very sharp like a sword.

The Practice that all is Hochma, &c; - made use of, by the above named four Kings, **Oriens**, **Paymon**, **Egyn** and **Amaymon**, is as followeth.

First, the four Kings, and their Particular Presidential Councillors, when directly Called upon, from their Several & respective Orders or mansions, to send such a spirit as was Nominated &c: to effect & fulfil all such proposals, as should be demanded, all which is thus.

O thou great & potent spirit Oriens, King of the East, & bearing Rule & Command In the East Region of the Air, I

---

[127] Baron, in Folger MS Vb 26, may be the root of Baroson.

adjure, call upon & Constrain, and most powerfully and Earnestly urge you, by & in, and through the virtue power & might of these Efficacious & binding names, **Tetragrammaton**, **Jehovah**, **Adonay**, **Agla**, **El**, **Sabaoth**, **Elohim**, Even the Almighty, Immense Incomprehensible & Everliving God, the omnipotent Creator of heaven & Earth, & in & through the names of our Lord & Saviour **Jesus Christ**, **Messias**, **Sother**, **Emanuel**, the only Begotten Son of god the father, born of the Virgin Mary, the High King & Lord of all the world, whose name all the Celestial Angels honour & obey, and before whom all the holy Company and Choir of heaven, Incessantly Sing **O Mappa laman Hallelujah** and at whose Divine & inestimable name, all Knees on Earth do homage and bow, and all the Aerial terrestrial and Infernal spirits Do fear & tremble,

And now by all aforesaid I do now again powerfully adjure, call upon, constrain & most Earnestly urge you O you great & mighty spirit **Oriens**, King of the East Quadrant of the Air, in and through the most Effectual glorious Sacred & puissant names of him who sayeth it is Done, that now Immediately without further tarrying, or delay, you do Send or Cause to be Sent forth without delay the spirit, **Marage** or any other from your Order, and to appear visibly, plainly, peaceably, affably in all serenity and humility here apparently to my Sight and view, and positively effectually faithfully, and fully to serve me and to Resolve me in such Queries, & Interrogations, as I Shall ask require & Demand of him, & to fulfil my Requests, and Do my Commandments in all things, according to his office, wherein he may or can, as I shall desire of him, & that without any Delay, Guile, Deceit or other illusions whatsoever, that may In any wise hinder, oppose, obstruct or destroy our Expectations. And I do again Earnestly

*Importune, adjure, Urge and Constrain you, O you powerful & Regal spirit **Oriens**, to send forthwith immediately, and now at this present time to me, and to appear plainly Visible before me, the spirit **Marage**, or some other from your orders or mansions, in all mildness, peace & friendliness, without any hurt, Disturbance, or any other Evil whatsoever, Either to me, or this place, wherein I am, or any other place, Person or creature whatsoever, but that Quietly Courteously & obediently to serve me & fulfil my Desires, & do my Commandments in all things wherein he may, &c: All which I Earnestly Urge & Constrain thee, O thou Royal and potent spirit **Oriens**: to do for me in Nomine Patri Filius et Spiritus Sancti.*

Let this Constraint be uttered three times, then proceed to the following Exorcism, and Say that Seven or nine times, then Go again to that above, which order observe for two or three hours, or as Occasion shall Require &c:

*O thou spirit **Marage**, I adjure, call upon, bind Constrain and Command thee by the Authority & Dignity of thy prince & head of thy Hierarchy, unto whom thou owest honour & obedience, & by the truest and most Especial name of your master, Commanding the Order and mansion wherein you Inhabit & Reside, I do adjure, Command, constrain & Earnestly urge thee, O thou spirit **Marage**, to appear, and show thy Self Visibly and affably in all Serenity & meekness here before me, in a fair & Decent form, and in no wise turbulent, hurtful or terrible unto me, or the place wherein I am, or to any other place or Creature whatsoever, or where such Places come you peaceably, & in all humility, & show thy Self plainly & visibly here before me, to my full view & Eye sight, speaking plainly, & to be understood, giving me faithful & free true answers to all my demands and readily doing my*

Command according to your office, wherein you may or Can, without any Illusion, or other fraudulent Deceptions whatsoever that lead to the Circumvention of my present Experiment or at all in the Least Destructive to my hopes and Expectations, move therefore, prepare ye & Come away, Show thy self, and make no long tarrying or Delay, and Do for me as for the Servant of the Highest.

	Paymon		West		Mirage[128]
and	Egyn	King of	North	be invocated,	or Baal
if		the		bid him send	Merage
	Amaymon		South		Marage

Now by Changing the names of the spirits, and the Angle from whence they are Called upon, Respect being had to the other three, as is Exemplified in the Regal spirit **Oriens**, whose Invocation in this last Experiment of my Hochma, may Serve also for those that are just next foregoing, and to be placed before the Invocation of the spiritual messenger **Temel**, and that of **Paymon**, to go before the Constraint of **Alphasis**, and the Invocation of **Amaymon**, to proceed the Call of **Emlon**, so that altering each name in Every several and respective Invocation, and observing the Aerial Angle, or Quarter, East, West, North, & South, & so Invocating according to art, you Can rarely Err or Do amiss &c.

There are other names, by which these four regal Spirits are Known, & have been Invoked, & been brought to familiarity & verbal Community by the L:C:E of S as:

---

[128] Mirage is described as another name for Sathan in Munich CLM 849.

Oriens		East		Orias	by the	Samael
Paimon	King	West	alias	Paymon	Hebrews	Azazel
Egyn	of	North		Egym	they are	Azael
Amaymon	the	South		Mayrary	called	Maharuel

Appendixes

Appendix 1: The Spirit Contract for Padiel

*I a Presidential Spirit by name called **Padiel**, residing & serving under **Carnesiel** a King of the Angle or Mansion of the West, at the Command of the Sovereign head of my Orders, and on my own accord, by the virtue power & force of Invocation on that behalf, do firmly & solidly bind & oblige my self by these present, Visibly to appear, in fair & decent Form, unto A:B and C:D[129] or either of them, at all times & in all places, whensoever & wheresoever, I shall of them, or either of them [be] called forth & moved thereunto; either in a Glass Receptacle* or otherwise out of it, as the Condition or Occasion of any matters in question or Operation shall properly or necessarily require.*

*And I the said Spirit **Padiel**, do also yet further & more especially bind & oblige myself, unto A:B & C:D or either of them as aforesaid, in by & through the truest & most especial name of my God, & by the principal head of my Orders, & by his Seal & Character & the virtue thereof, at the sight of which all Spirits in their several & respective degrees, Orders & Offices, do therein accordingly serve, honour & obey.*

And chiefly by this my Seal or Character, as here under is by me affixed or inserted. And by the force and virtue of these words most powerfully in the Sophick or Magick Art, **Lay, Alzym, Mura, Syron, Nalgava, Rythin, Layaganum,**

---

[129] A:B and C:D are abbreviations for people's names.

***Layarazin**, **Lasai**, By the content hereof, & by the virtue power & efficacy of all aforesaid, I the said Spirit **Padiel** do firmly & faithfully promise to appear visibly unto A:B & C:D: or either of them, in manner & form as aforesaid, & to make true & faithful answers, unto all & every their or either of their demands & requests, speaking plainly, & to be understood of them or either of them, & also readily, willingly & effectually to fulfil, perform & accomplish, all & every such their or either of their Commandments, as at any time they or either of them shall request & enjoin me, at all times & in all places, whensoever & wheresoever I shall of them or either of them moved, or called forth to visible appearance, during their or either of their natural lives, even to the last or ultimate Survivors. In testimony whereof being commanded, I have hereunto & hereunder, affixed or inserted, my true Seal or Character, unto which I serve & bear obedience, and have always stuck close.*[130]

*as being one usual manner of appearance & of receiving and enclosing of Spirits.

---

[130] Fo 71-71b

Bibliography

Bibliography – MSS

    Folger MS Vb26
    John Rylands GB 0133 Eng MS 40
    Rawlinson D1363
    Sloane MS 3821
    Sloane MS 3824
    Sloane MS 3825
    Wellcome MS 3203

Bibliography – Printed Sources

    Agrippa, H.C.; *The Fourth Book of Occult Philosophy*; 1978; Askin Publishers; London

    Anon; *The Black Pullet: Science of Magical Talisman*; 1972; Samuel Weiser Inc; New York

    Beard, C.R.; *The Romance of Treasure Trove*; 1933; Sampson Low & Co; London

    Briggs, K.M.; *Some Seventeenth-Century Books of Magic*; 1953; in *Folklore* 64.4:445-62

    Butler, E.M.; *Ritual Magic*; 1980; Cambridge University Press; Cambridge

    Casaubon, Meric (ed); *A True and Faithful Relation of what passed for many Years between Dr John Dee ... and some Spirits*; 1974; Askin Publishers; London, 1974

De Abano, Peter; *The Heptameron or Magical Elements*; 1978; in *The Fourth Book of Occult Philosophy*; Askin Publishers; London

Fanger, Claire (ed); *Conjuring Spirits: Texts and Traditions of Medieval Ritual Magic*; 1998; Pennsylvania State University Press; Pennsylvania

Grinsell, L.V.; *Barrow Treasure, in Fact, Tradition, and Legislation*; 1967; in *Folklore* 78.1:1-38.

Hamill, John (ed); *The Rosicrucian Seer: Magical Writings of Frederick Hockley*; 1986; Aquarian Press; Wellingborough

Kieckhefer, Richard; *Magic in the Middle Ages*; 2001; Cambridge University Press; Cambridge

Kieckhefer, Richard; *Forbidden Rites: A Necromancer's Manual of the Fifteenth Century*; 1997; Sutton Publishing; Stroud

Mowat, Barbara A.; *Prospero's Book*; 2001; in *Shakespeare Quarterly* 52.1:1-33; Folger Shakespeare Library; Washington

Paracelsus; *The Archidoxes of Magic*; 1975; Askin Publishers; London

Peterson, Joseph H. (ed); *The Lesser Key of Solomon*; 2001; Weiser Books; Maine

Peterson, Joseph H. (ed, trans); *Grimorium Verum*; 2007; CreateSpace; California

Peterson, Joseph H. (ed); *The Sixth and Seventh Books of Moses*; 2008; Ibis Press; Florida

Scot, Reginald; *The Discoverie of Witchcraft*; 1990; Dover Publications

Skinner, Stephen, & Rankine, David; *The Goetia of Dr Rudd*; 2007; Golden Hoard Press; Singapore

Skinner, Stephen, & Rankine, David; *The Keys to the Gateway of Magic*; 2005; Golden Hoard Press; Singapore

Skinner, Stephen, & Rankine, David; *The Practical Angel Magic of Dr John Dee's Enochian Tables*; 2004; Golden Hoard Press; Singapore

Thomas, Keith; *Religion and the Decline of Magic*; 1973; Penguin Books Ltd; Middlesex

Thompson, C.J.S.; *Mysteries and Secrets of Magic*; 1927; John Lane; London

Thorndike, Lynn; *A History of Magic and Experimental Science*; 1923; Columbia University Press; New York

Timbs, John; *Romance of London: Strange Stories, Scenes and Remarkable Persons of the Great Town*; 1865; Richard Bentley; London

Turner, Dawson; *On Treasure-Trove and Invocation of Spirits*; 1846; in *Norfolk Archaeology* 1:46-64

Waite, A.E.; *The Book of Black Magic and Ceremonial Magic*; 1973; Causeway Books; New York

Waite, A.E. (writing as Grand Orient); *Complete Manual of Occult Divination Volume 1*; 1972; University Books Inc; New York

Worms, Abraham von, & Dehn, Georg (ed), & Guth, Steven (trans); *The Book of Abramelin*; 2006; Ibis ress; Florida

Zietz, Stephen J. (ed); *Libellus Magicus: A Nineteenth Century Manuscript of Conjurations*; ND

Index

Africa 109, 110, 112
Agares 15, 16, 18, 32, 33, 35, 36, 37, 38, 39, 40, 42, 46, 145, 146, 147, 149, 150, 152, 154, 158, 159
Agrippa, Cornelius 15, 20, 22, 83, 94
Alicho 164
Alilgon 164
Alphasis 164, 168, 171
Alpherez 17, 138
Amaymon 55, 59, 60, 76, 139, 164, 167, 168, 171, 172
Anaboth 32, 33, 34, 36, 37, 38, 39, 40, 42, 46, 84, 87, 88, 89, 90, 164
Andromalius 16, 160
Art Almadel 17
Ashmole, Elias 20
Asmodai 16, 160
Azael 172
Azazel 172
Baal 51, 73, 164, 165, 171

Balferth 164
Balphares 15
Balserth 168
Baramper 17, 32, 33, 35, 36, 37, 38, 39, 40, 42, 46, 120, 123, 138
Barbaros 16, 32, 33, 34, 36, 37, 38, 39, 40, 42, 46, 84, 87, 88, 89, 90
Barbas 164
Barbasan 17, 33, 37, 46, 84, 87, 88, 89, 90, 120, 121, 123
Barbason 17, 33, 35, 36, 38, 39, 40, 42
Barbatos 16
Baro 142
Baroson 164, 168
Bealphares ... 17, 134, 137
Bealpharos 17, 134, 135, 139
Beelzebub 17, 20, 27, 28, 29, 59, 60, 65, 95, 162, 163

Belfarto 164, 166, 167, 168

Belferit .... *See* Belfarto

Belial 164, 168

Belknap, Sir Edward 11

Berith 164

Bileth ... 16, 156, *See* Bleth

Birto 14, 15, 131, 132, 133

Black Pullet 18

Bleth 16, 156, 158

Booth 131

Boytheon 55, 56, 58, 59, 61, 62, 64, 65

Bret .... *See* Brett

Brett 127, 130, 136

Camret 37, 39, 40, 42, 46, 88

Carnesiel 174

Causabon, Meric 16

Cerberus 96

Chalcos 32, 33, 34, 36, 37, 38, 39, 40, 42, 46, 84, 87, 88, 89, 90

Daemonologie 17

Dansiation 59, 60, 65

Dantalion 16, 160

de Abano, Peter 22

De Occulta Philosophia. 15, 94

Dee, Dr John 15, 16

Discoverie of Witchcraft 17, 134

Dragon 51, 133

Edward IV, King 14, 15, 131

Egym .... *See* Egyn

Egyn 55, 59, 60, 139, 164, 168, 171, 172

Elizabeth I, Queen 15

Emlon 164, 167, 171

Everges 32, 33, 35, 36, 37, 38, 39, 40, 42, 46, 84, 87, 88, 89, 90

Foca 109, 110, 112

Folger MS 2250 110

Folger MS Vb 26 15, 32, 109, 131, 164, 168

Folla 109, 110, 112

GB 0133 Eng MS 40 .... 15, 131, 134

Gijel 38, 39, 41, 42, 46, 89, 91

Goetia 15, 16, 22, 72, 74, 80, 154

Gordonizor 164

Gorson 16, 32, 33, 34, 36, 37, 38, 39, 40, 42, 46, 84, 87, 88, 89, 90

Gorzon .... *See* Gorson

Grimorium Verum 18

Henry VIII, King 11, 13

Heptameron 15, 20, 21, 22, 54, 68, 69, 74, 80
Hockley, Frederick 15, 140
James I, King 17
Janua Magica Reserata 19, 83
Jekyll, Sir Joseph 19, 20
Julia 109, 110, 112
Key of Solomon 18
Lamo 164
Lemegeton 19, 20, 71, 83
Libellus Magicus 17
Liber Juratus 15
Lilia 109, 110, 112, 113
Lilly, William 12
Lucifer 17, 20, 27, 28, 29, 59, 60, 65, 162
Madicon 164, 167
Madzilodarp 16, 49
Maharuel 172
Mala 164
Mamon 159
Marage 169, 170, 171
Mayerion 55, 56, 58, 59, 60, 61, 62, 64, 65
Mayrary See Amaymon
Mirage 171
Munich CLM 849 . 17, 171
Mureril 32, 33, 35, 36, 37, 38, 39, 40, 42, 46, 84, 87, 88, 89, 90
Mycob 109, 110

Neophryn 164
Nine Keys 19
Oberion 11, 13, 109
Ocarbidaton 164, 167
Ophis 94
Orias See Oriens
Oriens 55, 59, 60, 139, 163, 164, 165, 166, 167, 168, 169, 171, 172
Ornotheos 131
Othry 164
Padiel 18, 147, 174, 175
Paracelsus 17
Pauline Art 20
Paymon 55, 59, 60, 139, 164, 167, 168, 171, 172
Pluto 96
Plyomn See Paymon
Ramblane See Rombulence
Roab 38, 39, 40, 42, 46, 89, 91
Rombulence 164, 168
Romulon 164
Rostilia 109, 110, 112
Rudd, Dr Thomas 19, 64
Rudd, John 64
Samael 172
Sathan 17, 20, 27, 28, 29, 59, 60, 65, 84, 87, 88, 89, 90, 120, 162, 163

Scarus.................. *See* Scor
Scor 38, 39, 40, 42, 46, 89, 91
Scot, Reginald 17, 134, 137
Seere..................... 16, 159
Serapis......................... 96
Shakespeare, William ... 17
Sibley, Ebenezer........... 15
Sixth and Seventh Books of Moses....................... 18
Sloane MS 3821 19
Sloane MS 3824 14, 15, 16, 17, 19, 20, 22, 147
Sloane MS 3825 15, 19, 20, 21, 71, 72, 83, 97, 109
Sloane, Sir Hans 19, 20
Sobarbas..................... 164
Somers, Baron John..... 20
Sondama.................... 161
Sondanna.... *See* Sondama
Sonenel 32, 33, 34, 36, 37, 38, 39, 40, 42, 46, 84, 87, 88, 89, 90
Sonoryan.................... 158
Spatula 148, 149
Sperion 55, 56, 58, 59, 60, 61, 62, 64, 65
Stapleton, William 13
Sulpher .... *See* Sulphur

Sulphur 32, 33, 34, 36, 37, 38, 39, 40, 42, 46, 84, 87, 88, 89, 90
Temell 64, 165, 166, 167, 168, 171
Theltrion 59, 61, 62, 64, 65
Theltryon.......... 55, 56, 58
Trithemius, Johannes . 20, 21, 22
True and Faithful Relation 16
Turner, Robert 16, 21, 71, 72
Um........................... 164
Umbra 38, 39, 40, 42, 46, 89, 91
Urinuo............. *See* Oriens
Urinus............. *See* Oriens
Usago .... *See* Vassago
Vassago 15, 16, 18, 32, 33, 35, 36, 37, 38, 39, 40, 42, 46, 72, 84, 87, 88, 89, 90, 140, 141, 142, 143, 145, 149, 150, 152, 158, 159, 164
Venulla............... 110, 112
Wellcome MS 3203 15, 131
Wharton, Goodwin........ 14
Zaym 38, 39, 40, 42, 46, 89, 91